"In a world where [illegible] easy to become overworked at the office, overwhelmed at home, and overcome with the details of living, Debbie Griffiths' *Little Lady, BIG DREAM* is a breath of fresh air. Her book is transparent, encouraging, and insightful, offering help and hope for balancing the demands of life."

BABBIE MASON
Recording Artist, Author, Talk Show Host
www.babbie.com

"Debbie Griffiths allowed me one of the great 'aha' moments in my life when she shared her lifelong and divinely inspired dream to serve older people and to do so in loving care to the glory of God. The story she shared became a Technicolor vision of what could be! As I watched from the box seat of life, her dream sprang to life out of the Rose City soil. Southern Pines Retirement Community bloomed and stood unrivaled in Southwest Georgia."

HUGH ROCKETT
Director of Development
Baptist Village Retirement Communities

"All of us have a dream planted deep inside of us; a hidden desire to do something far beyond our perceived capabilities,experiences, and resources. Unfortunately, for most of us, our desire remains just that—a dream. The book you're holding in your hands strips away all of the standard excuses and calls us to chase our BIG DREAM. Debbie Griffiths has proven that past setbacks and current obstacles are no longer a valid excuse for casting our dreams away."

JOE COLAVITO
VP External Development
Wells Real Estate Funds.
Author, *Jelly Donut Junction... What's Inside Matters*

"Debbie Griffiths so poignantly shares the accomplishment of her Dream! Her journey was heart-rending, uplifting, inspirational, and personally challenging. I admire her greatly, her faith, focus, and finalization of her God-given Dream. It refreshed my memory that there are yet goals and dreams in my life to be worked on and brought to fruition. It is with renewed faith and determination that I pursue some unfinished dreams in my life."

Norma Turner
The Marina Cathedral
Los Angeles, California

"Reading *Little Lady, BIG DREAM* is like visiting with a friend, a friend who trusts you with intimate details of her life—her pain, her passions, and her faith in God, faith that propelled her to accomplish her big dream and His will! What an amazing testimony to the promise that 'all things work together for good to them that love God' (Romans 8:28 KJV)."

Sandra W. Haymon, Ph.D.
Psychologist
Author, *My Turn, Caring for Aging Parents*
Tallahassee, Florida

"What an amazing book; a truly inspiring read for me! I could not put this book down. The author's accomplishments and drive are utterly remarkable. The scriptures and quotes are a tremendous blessing and encouragement for me as I pursue my 'dream.' Southern Pines Retirement Community has got to be spectacular... Some day, when traveling in Georgia, I will stop in Thomasville to see Southern Pines for myself."

Char Anderson
Hand-in-Hand Ministries
Jupiter, Florida

"*Little Lady, BIG DREAM* is a wonderful example of how hard work, determination, and faith in God and in oneself enables individuals to live their dreams—even Big Dreams. This is a powerful and emotionally charged true story that will grip your heart."

Patty Rubino Brunetti
Chairman Board of Directors
Valley View Packing Company Inc.
San Jose, California

"What an honest, inspiring, touching, interesting, heart-warming, and informative read! This ... is a testimony to the power of faith and holding fast to an uncompromising belief in your dream!"

Joy Broome
Dietary Manager
Magnolia Place
Cairo, Georgia

"There is so much within the pages of Debbie's 'life.' Many will receive blessing and encouragement from her personal and business testimony. With the many heartaches and obstacles she faced, she never took her focus from Him. It is evident that God has blessed her faithfulness as she certainly overcame serious tests within her years."

Evelyn Borschel
Tallahassee, Florida

"What a wonderful, well-written book. There are so many things that I loved about it, including all the quotes and Bible verses sprinkled within the pages. I deeply admired the author's love of the elderly. I also admired her husband and son for not only supporting her, but for jumping in and being involved. It was interesting to read what all planning, starting, building, and running a business like Southern Pines entails. I appreciated her honesty in the book of what it cost her spiritually, physically, and emotionally to run the retirement community with her workaholic tendencies. Her honesty gives readers a lot to think about and will hopefully encourage them to use their gifts within God's framework of design."

Janet Wilfred,
President
Pine Blossoms Website Designs
Moultrie, Georgia

Debbie Griffiths has effortlessly achieved something rare in literature: She has given us an unobstructed view into the human heart. The challenges she faced and the victories won are so very personal, yet universal, that each moment of her story unites and reminds us of our shared humanity. This story will echo long after the last page has been read. It's a reminder that each lifetime is a series of events, and we can color and shape these events with endless love, ferocious courage, and undying hope.

Michael McClendon,
Screenwriter/Director

# Little Lady, BIG DREAM

DREAM BIG!

Proverbs 16:3

Debbie Griffiths

# Little Lady, BIG DREAM

DEBBIE GRIFFITHS R.N.C

ONE LIFE LOST IN A TRAGIC ACCIDENT,
ANOTHER ONE FOUND IN SERVICE TO OTHERS

This title is also available as a Tate Out Loud product. Visit www.tatepublishing.com for more information.



Published by Tate Publishing & Enterprises, LLC
127 E. Trade Center Terrace | Mustang, Oklahoma 73064 USA
1.888.361.9473 | www.tatepublishing.com

Tate Publishing is committed to excellence in the publishing industry. The company reflects the philosophy established by the founders, based on Psalm 68:11,
*"The Lord gave the word and great was the company of those who published it."*


*Edited by Kylie Lyons*
*Cover design by Kandi Evans*
*Interior design by Kellie Southerland*

Published in the United States of America

ISBN: 978-1-62902-343-4
1. Christian Living: Business Relationships/Personal Growth
2. Biography & Autobiography: Personal Memoirs/Business Life: Inspirational
13.08.19

# This book is dedicated to...

Each *resident* who lovingly made the choice to live under my roof during the twenty years I ministered as a long-term care provider in my hometown.

Each *employee* who willingly ministered alongside me as we tenderly met the needs of hundreds of residents at Camellia Gardens, Mulberry Place, and Southern Pines.

*Older Americans...*
*Our Greatest Natural Resource*

*In Memory Of:*
Miss Lucille
Miss Ruth

# Don't Regret Growing Old—It's a Privilege Denied to Many

"Do not cast me away when I am old; do not
forsake me when my strength is gone."
Psalm 71:9

# Acknowledgments

I would like to express my sincere thanks to all those who helped in the various phases of this project:

To Dr. Tim Morrison, President of Write-Choice Services, who started me in the right direction; his encouragement and support showed me early on that I did have a story to tell. While editing my material, he made sure my voice, my passion, and my vision came through in my writing.

To Nancy Arant Williams, a retired registered nurse, who edited my material and bonded with me in a caring way while providing valuable advice. When I got stuck, she came up with the right concepts to get me going again.

To my mother, who answered my endless questions and helped jog my memory so that I could accurately share my story; she understood the tug on my heart to write this book in hopes of encouraging others to follow their dreams.

To my brother, Danny, and my sister-in-law, Rehberg,

who had faith in my "second" dream; their encouragement helped me to not only start this book, but to finish it as well.

To Wanda Sons, my friend and sister in Christ, who read my manuscript and shared her unique perspective.

To the scores of friends who offered their love and encouragement as my idea developed into this book.

How do I adequately thank my husband and my son? Not only did they love and support me through the building of a premier retirement community, but also through the endless hours of writing so I could share my life story—or at least the first fifty years.

To Michael McClendon, screenwriter & director (*Little Lady, BIG DREAM*, The Movie) who confirmed that my story was worthy and took it on a journey to the big screen.

Above all, to my heavenly Father, who gave me the courage to share intimate details of my life journey so others can clearly see: "God uses ordinary people to do extraordinary things!"

# Contents

"Come and listen, all you who fear God; let me tell you what He has done for me."
*Psalm 66:16*


Foreword . . . . . . . . . . . . . . . . . . . . . . . . . . . . . .17
Author's Note . . . . . . . . . . . . . . . . . . . . . . . . . . .19
My Version of Psalm 23 . . . . . . . . . . . . . . . . . . . . .21
I Have to Go Now!. . . . . . . . . . . . . . . . . . . . . . . . .23
Where Did I Come From? . . . . . . . . . . . . . . . . . . . .33
Trouble On the Home Front . . . . . . . . . . . . . . . . . .43
Safe on the Farm . . . . . . . . . . . . . . . . . . . . . . . . .51
Shy Girl... With a Vision . . . . . . . . . . . . . . . . . . .57
I Am Someone Special! . . . . . . . . . . . . . . . . . . . . .65
Wedding Plans in the Air. . . . . . . . . . . . . . . . . . . .75
A Life-Changing Phone Call. . . . . . . . . . . . . . . . . .83
Letting Go of the House . . . . . . . . . . . . . . . . . . . .97
Finding Purpose After Loss. . . . . . . . . . . . . . . . . .103

The Man I Call Bo . . . . . . . . . . . . . . . . . . . . . . . . . . 115
Call to Long-Term Care . . . . . . . . . . . . . . . . . . . . . . . . 127
Call to Senior Adult Ministry . . . . . . . . . . . . . . . . . . 137
Oncology, This Is Debbie . . . . . . . . . . . . . . . . . . . . . 141
The Mulberry Family . . . . . . . . . . . . . . . . . . . . . . . . . 145
The Yellow Envelope . . . . . . . . . . . . . . . . . . . . . . . . . 159
The Toughest Choice . . . . . . . . . . . . . . . . . . . . . . . . . 165
Location, Location, Location . . . . . . . . . . . . . . . . . . 173
Start-up Ain't Easy . . . . . . . . . . . . . . . . . . . . . . . . . . 179
Million-Dollar Dream . . . . . . . . . . . . . . . . . . . . . . . . 187
Multimillion-Dollar Dream . . . . . . . . . . . . . . . . . . . . 201
With Dreams Come Heartaches . . . . . . . . . . . . . . . . 213
Above and Beyond . . . the Call . . . . . . . . . . . . . . . . 223
Work, Work, Work . . . . . . . . . . . . . . . . . . . . . . . . . . . 233
Making the Big Decision . . . . . . . . . . . . . . . . . . . . . 239
The Longest Year . . . . . . . . . . . . . . . . . . . . . . . . . . . 249
Early Retirement . . . . . . . . . . . . . . . . . . . . . . . . . . . 261
In God's Will at RoosterVille . . . . . . . . . . . . . . . . . 269
Little Lady, BIG DREAM . . . . . . . . . . . . . . . . . . . . . 275
Move, Move, Move . . . . . . . . . . . . . . . . . . . . . . . . . . 281
Speechless . . . . . . . . . . . . . . . . . . . . . . . . . . . . . . . . . 289
RoosterVille . . . Letting Go . . . . . . . . . . . . . . . . . . . 299
The Lavender Book . . . . . . . . . . . . . . . . . . . . . . . . . 305
Legacy Of Faith . . . . . . . . . . . . . . . . . . . . . . . . . . . . 313
Epilogue: My Version of Psalm 30 . . . . . . . . . . . . . . 319
Afterword . . . . . . . . . . . . . . . . . . . . . . . . . . . . . . . . . 321
Work Addiction Self-Test . . . . . . . . . . . . . . . . . . . . . 323

# Foreword

Debbie Griffiths allowed me one of the great "aha" moments in my life when she shared her lifelong and divinely inspired dream to serve older people and to do so in loving care to the glory of God. The story she shared became a Technicolor vision of what could be!

How exciting the next few years were! As I watched from the box seat of life, her dream sprang to life out of the Rose City soil. Southern Pines Retirement Community bloomed and stood unrivaled in Southwest Georgia.

By faith, Debbie grabbed opportunity, and with God's guidance and others' confirmation, her dream became a blessing to individuals, families, and spilled over into the whole community.

Reverend Hugh Rockett
Director of Development
Baptist Village Retirement Communities

# Author's Note

A Spiritual Memoir—a life story... filled with amazing illustrations of God's hand at work...

A story of faith, obedience, guidance, determination, perseverance, forgiveness, compassion and... ultimately success—in the midst of what seemed like an impossibility.

A Love Story... Two Love Stories... with unfailing love and devotion easily recognizable.

While reading this book, it might be easy to have a negative reaction to some individuals and events. However, my genuine prayer is that as you finish the book in its entirety, you will be able to clearly see how God used all of these circumstances to mold us into the individuals He intended for us each to become.

Some of the names in this book have been changed in order to maintain the dignity and privacy of others. While I have tried to remember events and conversations to the best of my ability, quotation marks are not necessarily an indication that the words appearing in quotes are exact.

# Introduction

## My Version of Psalm 23

The Lord is my owner and my director,
I shall not question His leadership.
He expects me to fully obey His commandments.
He leads me to make the right decisions.
He gives me inner peace,
He shows me His plan for my life
that His name might be glorified.
Although I live in a world of much
evil and uncertainty,
I will not fret or lose hope,
for my God is always with me.
His Presence and His support
shall always uplift me.
He gave me a strong and sincere
desire to minister to senior adults,
He planned my life and my career for me
in the presence of my family, my residents,
and my staff.

Oh, how joy and contentment overflow as I
seek to follow His Will.
Surely wisdom and peace shall follow me
all the days of my life.
And I shall sit at the feet of my owner
and my director forever.

# Chapter 1

## I Have to Go Now!

"Far and away the best prize that life offers is the chance to work hard at work worth doing."
*Theodore Roosevelt*

**Monday, June 13, 2005**

From the time I left work at five p.m., we wondered how many last-minute phone calls we would get before it was all over. During those final hours, we sat in our living room anxiously awaiting one more phone call for Bo to repair a toilet or for me to fill in for another no-show.

After watching the eleven o'clock news, we made our way to our bedroom. "Just as sure as I get ready for bed," Bo said, "I'll have to get dressed again."

We climbed into bed, propped our heads on a double set of pillows, and watched our clock tick away the minutes. At 11:55, we began counting down: five minutes, four minutes, three minutes, two minutes, one minute, fifty seconds, forty seconds, thirty seconds, twenty seconds, ten seconds, midnight. Only then did we allow ourselves a huge sigh of relief.

Bo turned on his side and pulled me close to him, nuzzling his head next to mine. I felt his heart beat as well as the warmth of his breath. His tender embrace assured me that I wasn't simply dreaming. It had really happened! A few minutes later he turned out the bedside lamp. We fell asleep whispering, "Free at last."

For Bo, that midnight chime signified a new beginning. He was about to regain me, his wife, his soul mate, and full-time bed partner after a ten-year loan to a business I dearly loved. Spending endless hours at home alone, Bo had longed for this day. In just a few hours, we would be free of legal entanglements and be a family once again.

For Kyle, our only son, now in his junior year of college, the chime meant having his mom back, free and available, finally, with all the time in the world for him.

### Tuesday, June 14, 2005

Awakened by the sound of an alarm clock ringing at six a.m., Bo rolled out of bed in full anticipation of the day we thought would never come. For the past hour, I had lain awake, waiting for the alarm to sound. The excitement of the day's events, which included the two p.m. closing of the sale, had kept me tossing and turning all night.

As I crawled out of bed, I recognized a familiar emotion churning deep within me: that gnawing emptiness that occurs when one loses a loved one. We call it grief. I knew that feeling all too well throughout my life, beginning with losing my first love nearly thirty years earlier. Now, letting go of my business had created a similar feeling of loss.

Needing the comfort of familiar things, I dressed in my

favorite ladybug frock and red shoes. Like a third party, I watched my emotions vacillate from melancholy to ecstasy as I made the drive alone to Albany, Georgia, for the closing. Bo decided to remain in town, on standby, tending to my mother, who was hospitalized and on the verge of emergency surgery.

As I drove, I quietly thought of how the day's events would change my life:

> *Today is Flag Day, but for me it's the most important day of my life.*
>
> *A myriad of emotions stir deep within me as I come face-to-face with the reality. Today is my last day as owner of Southern Pines Retirement Community. After today, I can no longer claim the title of "Miss Southern Pines."*
>
> *This change means more than merely releasing the eight-plus acres of land, two spacious buildings, and four charming Victorian cottages to their new owners. I am also letting go of the passion that was born over twenty years ago.*
>
> *Today I am satisfying my guarantee, keeping a promise when I drive to the bank to pay off the mortgage balance. What an awesome sense of personal satisfaction!*
>
> *I feel sad to leave the loving family of residents and staff at Southern Pines. Today I leave behind a part of myself. The legal world calls it goodwill. I call it blood, sweat, and tears.*

Soon I would sit flanked by my closing attorneys in a conference room, and I would sign the documents to relinquish ownership of Southern Pines—my baby—after giving it my heart, soul, and strength for ten straight years.

For legal reasons, Bo and I had agreed at the outset to keep our personal and business lives separate, putting it in my name alone. Nonetheless, Bo had been there, supportive and completely involved since its inception. Though his contribution had been enormous and indispensable, I alone would sign on the dotted line.

As I entered the lawyer's office, I was greeted by a member of my team of attorneys, who escorted me to a spacious gathering room. A stack of paperwork lay on a long mahogany table. Those papers awaited my signature. My heart pumped rapidly as the magnitude of the moment swept over me.

Greeting me with a firm handshake and a warm pat on the back, attorney Ralph Rodgers asks, "Well, Debbie, how do you feel today?" I knew he understood my feelings. His Aunt Doris had been a resident at Southern Pines for the past five years.

He smiled. "My family and I will never forget your loyalty and dedication, Debbie. We appreciate all the fabulous activities you planned for the residents over the years. I know Doris enjoyed each and every one."

"Thank you, Ralph. It was my pleasure." At that moment, I struggled to hold back tears. I was relieved that neither Bo nor my partners had come to the closing with me. Familiarity might have made the struggle more difficult than it was.

Ralph and his legal partners had worked alongside me since the original "Intent to Purchase" documents were signed nearly nine months earlier. The complexity of the sale with all the legalities combined with the various local and state licensing board requirements had delayed the closing until now. The delay had sapped what little emotional and physical reserve I had, and today I could truthfully say, "I'm ready to sign."

After the paperwork was finished, Ralph stood to present me with a check to complete the sale. In closing the deal, I had fulfilled my lifelong dream of becoming a successful female entrepreneur.

Although the closing conference was completed in less than an hour, the stack of paperwork seemed endless. It was a vivid reminder of my first days at the bank when I, a middle-income geriatric nurse with a dream, unbelievingly and boldly borrowed the first million dollars. In some ways, the closing was similar to those early days. However, from an emotional standpoint, it was altogether different. In time, my initial excitement in making my dream real became an exercise in perpetual exhaustion. Even though I was ready to move on, letting go of my dream was emotionally gut wrenching.

Following the closing events, at my request, the lawyers joined me in posing for photographs. Ralph requested a duplicate for his files.

My supportive mother, who had always been skeptical of my entrepreneurial spirit, told me she wondered how I slept at night while being responsible for such an enormous debt. Today I proved to the whole world, including my mom and myself, I not only started my commission well, but I finished it well.

As I drove away from the law firm in the company van and headed back to Thomasville, I pondered again the finality of the transaction. This was my last trip in one of the three company vehicles that now belonged to Southern Pines' new owners.

For a brief moment, my thoughts raced back to the days

when I shopped for the two white Dodge Caravans. One I procured locally, while the other I drove back from North Carolina. Then I recalled all the deliberation that went into the purchase of the third vehicle—a Park Avenue car. We deemed the car necessary for those residents not able to maneuver in and out of the vans.

Never was there a time away from Southern Pines that I wasn't constantly aware of the needs of my business. With one hundred residents, a seventy-member staff, and a minimum of three hundred family members, I carried a heavy load. My mind could scarcely comprehend the significant change that had resulted from the stroke of a pen.

Driving along the Georgia-Florida parkway, I thought about my residents and staff, who were also experiencing change. Change provokes feelings of uncertainty and even anxiety for everyone involved. I quietly prayed for them as I had many times over the past months.

Although my ultimate desire was for a church-affiliated group to purchase Southern Pines, I felt satisfied knowing I had chosen new owners who would continue my mission. In time, I knew everything would be all right for the residents and the staff.

Suddenly, I recalled the day my bankers joined me for a farewell appreciation lunch at Southern Pines. They had been as zealous as I in making my dream come true. We posed together for a photo that would also serve as a reminder of the giant risk I had taken to start a business.

Then I remembered all the photo albums I had assembled during my tenure. With the updated resident and employee pictures, I had filled a dozen scrapbooks with precious visual memories. Early in the game, I had asked the attorneys to itemize in the Purchase Agreement a list of various sentimental pieces I planned to take with me.

The photo albums topped my list. In the coming weeks and months, even years, these photos will re-tell the story of my life and my work at Southern Pines.

The teapots above the cabinets in the dining room, the unique cream-colored Victorian settee in my office, and the original display signs used to promote Southern Pines were also tangible items I genuinely wanted as keepsakes. The old four-wheeled buggy and the replica cannon were at the top of Bo's wish list. We were relieved when, without the slightest hesitation, the buyers willingly and graciously honored our requests.

Thirty-five miles down the road, as I entered Mitchell County, I realized I couldn't make it back to deposit the check before the bank closed at four p.m. I didn't want to hold that check for any length of time.

Grabbing my cell phone from my purse, I quickly made a call to the bank, "Mr. Stephen Cheney, please." Within a second Mr. Cheney, bank president, listened as I explained my dilemma.

"I will not officially close the bank until you arrive, so take your time, Debbie," he said. "I'll keep a teller line open and we'll tally the day's transactions after your visit." In an instant, that moment sparked a gentle reminder of the valuable business relationships and support I had garnered over the years. Mr. Cheney had confirmed the fact one more time.

At 4:25, I arrived at the bank and quickly made my way up the stairs. I was given a royal welcome and assisted with my bank transaction, just as would have happened any ordinary day. As the teller handed me the deposit slip, she asked a question that piqued the interest of others standing nearby. "Debbie, what do you plan to do now that you've retired?"

Having replied to that question many times in past months, I answered without hesitation. "After I 'find myself' again, I plan to write a book in hopes of encouraging others to follow their dreams. I'll probably name it 'Little Lady, BIG DREAM.'"

"I can hardly wait to read that book!" she said. "Just the title alone is so you." As I started to leave, I was immediately surrounded by bank employees each sharing words of congratulations and sincere hugs.

Driving the van out of the bank parking lot, I realized I was still carrying one of the company's six handheld radio phones. More importantly, I still had the keys to Southern Pines in my purse. Since I couldn't make it back to the facility before five o'clock, I decided to wait until the next day to return the items I used many times as owner and executive director.

Shortly after 5:30 p.m., I parked the white Dodge Caravan in the facility parking lot, got into my white Chrysler Town and Country van, and drove across the street to Puzzle Lake. As I began to unwind, one thing struck me: I was no longer on-call. That fact alone removed a huge weight from my shoulders!

By that time, I was bone-weary and totally convinced it was time for me to move on. The back property, still undeveloped, was primed and in dire need of its fifth expansion. But somehow none of these facts made the day any less traumatic for me. Like a mother with her newborn baby, only I could know the real attachment I had so reluctantly relinquished.

Before pulling into the garage, I took one final glance

across the way at Southern Pines before parking the van and heading into the house. Peering through the kitchen window, I could see Bo sitting in the swing on the back porch, but as much as I wanted to join him, I desperately needed the next few minutes alone.

As I stood facing the bathroom mirror, I recalled the nonstop events of the hectic day. I couldn't help but smile as tears of joy misted in my eyes. The passion and the determination were evident from the very start. All our hard work, long hours, and perseverance had finally paid off: The check was in the bank. It almost seemed too good to be true.

Then in a moment of gratefulness, away from it all, the tears began to dissipate as I stood quietly thanking God for His guidance and direction. *At the age of forty-eight, this young chick was ready to retire.*

---

"All changes, even the most longed for, have their melancholy, for what we leave behind us is a part of ourselves; we must die to one life before we can enter into another."
*Anatole France*

# Chapter 2

## Where Did I Come From?

"Before I was born the Lord called me; from my birth he has made mention of my name."
*Isaiah 49:1b*

Mama and Daddy married on September 17, 1952, and although this was a first marriage for Daddy, Mama had married her first husband, Jack, at age sixteen. Two years later, Jack and Mama had a son named Billy. When Billy was just two, Jack and Mama divorced. Then when Billy was almost five, Mama married my daddy, whose name was also Jack. Daddy often called Mama "Polly," short for Pauline.

Thirteen months after Daddy and Mama married, their first son, Danny, was born. Three years later I was born, and six years after that David became the baby of the family.

Mama was reared in a large family with one sister and seven brothers. She grew up in the small town of Coolidge, Georgia, and lacked one year finishing high school. Grandma and Grandpa were strict disciplinarians. Mama told me many times that she married early to be on her own.

Daddy was raised in a low-income family in Mitchell County, with five siblings. His parents forced him to quit school in the second grade to help provide for the family. Although Daddy was never able to return to school, he joined the navy during the Korean Conflict. How disappointed he was when after only four months of service bronchial asthma forced him to take a medical discharge. While most young men complained about military service, Daddy was delighted to serve his country because the military provided three meals a day—something he could never count on before.

Although Daddy had completed only two grades in school, he seldom let anything get the best of him. He did calculations in his head without pencil or paper. A detailed person, he always recorded in writing the date of any purchase he'd made. With his photographic memory, he recalled important events and was able to answer any family history question in an instant.

My parents lived in the housing projects on College Street when I was born the Sunday morning after Thanksgiving. I was nearly a month old before the neighbors realized Mama and Daddy had a new baby girl. Mama proudly named me after her movie idol, Debbie Reynolds.

Before I was six, we moved at least a half dozen times. I remember living in three different houses on Bartow Street, all within walking distance of each other. From Bartow Street to Rosedale Avenue to McIntyre Street, my parents were always looking for something better—a more perfect house with a better location.

Shortly after David was born, we moved to a new Jim

Walter home that Mama and Daddy had custom built on Raleigh Avenue. They were proud of their cherished dwelling: a three bedroom, one bath, framed home—the nicest accommodation either of them had ever had.

Later they added a charming white picket fence across the front of the yard and a chain link fence around the backyard to keep little brother from wandering off. Both of my parents became overly protective after David had a frightening bout with rheumatic fever. I remember repeated reminders to stay close to home.

Growing up with brothers, I was destined to be a tomboy. I enjoyed playing softball and could keep up with my brothers most any day. Neighborhood softball games always took place in our backyard.

I remember an afternoon when the neighborhood kids started throwing rocks. Danny saw a rock coming straight toward me. He yelled. I turned my head at the sound of Danny's yell. Just as I turned my head, I was hit directly above my right eye. Within minutes, Mama was on the scene, offering aid and comfort. Three hours later, I returned from the emergency room with a scar that remains to this day.

Danny and I often rode our bikes to Taylor's Grocery Store, nearly five blocks from our house, to purchase our favorite penny candies. As always, a strict time was set for us to return home.

One afternoon when Danny and I left Taylor's Store, we decided to cross Campbell Street so that we could ride our bikes over London Bridge—something we had always wanted to do. We boldly took a chance and survived and Mama never found out.

We also rode our bikes to Harper School. Mama insisted

we wait for the sound of the sawmill horn, a mile or so away from our house, before we could leave for school. When the horn sounded at eight a.m., we jumped on our bikes and made a beeline to the school. We had exactly twenty minutes to get to school before the tardy bell rang.

Mama never worked outside the home until the three of us were all in school. An industrious homemaker, she enjoyed cooking and sewing, making pant outfits and jumpers for me. I wore those outfits with pride. We didn't have expensive clothing, but we dressed to perfection, thanks to Mama. She believed in ironing everything: the bed sheets, pillow cases, even my brother's t-shirts.

The inside of our home was immaculate. Mama redecorated and rearranged the furniture so often that Daddy always turned on the lights whenever he arrived home late just in case Mama had rearranged things during the day. Daddy didn't want to accidentally wind up sitting on the floor.

I remember one summer Mama asked Daddy to relocate the kitchen sink, plumbing and all, from one side of the kitchen to the other. She was tired of the view of the backyard and wanted the sink to face the living room. Daddy was a great handyman, and he always aimed to please Mama. He couldn't understand, however, when she decided less than forty-eight hours later that she wanted the sink moved back to its original place. Clearly, Mama's changes always made our home look and feel more comfortable.

Just like Mama, Daddy appreciated a tidy house. He especially hated the dark rings that form in toilet bowls. "Get the bleach," he'd often say.

Being the only girl in my family, I learned by experience how to keep house. In fact, many of the obsessive tendencies that I developed as an adult stemmed from my early childhood training.

My best friend, Nancy, and I spent many nights together at each other's homes. Sheree, another close friend who lived in our neighborhood, often joined our pajama parties. Our teachers and friends sometimes referred to us as the "three musketeers."

Nancy's mom, Gloria, and my mama enjoyed visiting at each other's homes, sitting at the kitchen table drinking coffee and gossiping. Nancy's family lived on the other end of Raleigh Avenue, so we had a common thread—we both lived on the wrong side of the railroad tracks, as all of Raleigh Avenue was on the wrong side.

When Mama and Gloria met at our home, the minute the ladies finished their last sip of coffee I quickly washed the cups, wiped the table, and hung the mugs neatly in the cabinet.

"I wish my three girls were like that," Gloria remarked. "You see there, girls, Debbie is always cleaning the house." Those compliments always felt good. Besides, sitting idle had always been uncomfortable for me. I found it difficult to carry on a conversation without performing a task at the same time.

Every Monday night at 9:30, just thirty minutes after my bedtime, my favorite television show, "Family Affair," would come on. I remember sneaking out of bed and peeking around the corner, eager to see my program. If I heard Mama coming down the hall, I jumped back in bed and pretended to be asleep. Mama was a strict disciplinarian in every sense of the word.

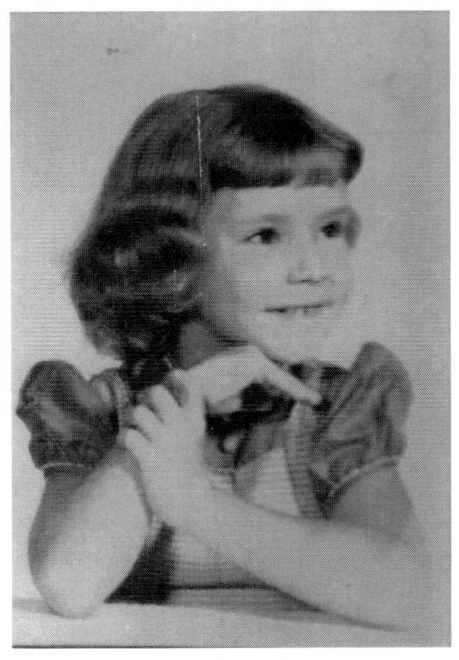

*First-grader at Harper School.*
*I was "blind as a bat" and didn't even know it!*

Midway through second grade, my teacher noticed I was having trouble seeing the blackboard. Dr. Blackman, our friend and optometrist, performed an exam and told Mama, "If your little girl was standing across the street from you, she could not recognize you as her mom." Dr. Blackman prescribed glasses and suggested the problem might have stemmed from a case of German measles I had contracted at age ten months. As much as I liked being able to see, I never liked wearing glasses.

I had a standing weekly appointment at the beauty shop, right along with Mama, to get my hair fixed—like mother, like daughter. One Thursday morning, Mama gave me permission to ride my blue Schwinn bicycle to Early and Late Beauty Nook, where she would meet me. I had nearly arrived when a ferocious brown Husky came running toward me and took a big bite out of my left lower leg. When I arrived at the beauty shop, blood was running down my leg. Shortly, a police officer arrived and a report was filed. Right then and there arrangements were made for the old dog to be tested and possibly euthanized. Listening to the shop full of ladies discussing the possibility of rabies injections in my abdomen, I was terrified. Fortunately, the rabies test came back negative.

Both of my parents loved country music, so it wasn't long before I learned to enjoy it as well. I remember the four-foot-wide oak stereo console with built-in dual speakers that sat in our living room. Many afternoons after school I loaded a dozen or more single records on the stereo turntable, and with my ear glued to the stereo speaker, I sang along for hours while listening to my favorite artists.

One of my favorite songs was "I've Been Everywhere," sung by Lynn Anderson. After a time I had memorized all the cities and states she mentioned in the song. Many of my school friends asked me to write the locations on paper. As a budding entrepreneur, I sold copies for a dime.

Early on our parents began teaching us the value of hard work. Danny and I earned spending money and bought school clothes and supplies with money we made from mowing neighbors' lawns and selling boiled peanuts. The work ethic we learned prepared us to be energetic workers with an intense sense of accomplishment.

My family and I loved our nightly outings to Pal's Drive-In. It resembled the modern-day Sonic and was just a few blocks from home, near the drive-in theater. Shortly before David was born, we went to Pal's nearly every night after supper. I always ordered chocolate milk, while Danny got a Coke, and our parents enjoyed after-dinner coffee while sitting in the car and visiting as a family. These are the memories I refer to as the "good ole days." To this day, one of my favorite pastimes is driving through the nearby neighborhoods. Unfortunately, Pal's doesn't exist anymore, so our new favorite location is Dairy Queen.

As far back as I can remember we took yearly vacations. The Smoky Mountains of North Carolina, from Ghost Town in Maggie Valley to Unto These Hills in Cherokee, were among our favorite destinations. Sometimes we traveled to Florida, enjoying excursions to Six Gun Territory, Silver Springs, and Disney World. We always had a great time once we left home, but for a week prior to the departure date, we were unsure if we were really going since Mama and Daddy fussed and argued until late evening on the night before we planned to leave. I remember repeatedly begging Mama, "Please, let's take our vacation as we planned."

Christmas was always a big event at our house. We each made a detailed wish list, and Mama made sure we got most of the items on our lists. On Christmas Eve there was an abundance of gifts under the tree. Although Daddy never complained about Mama buying gifts, he never participated in the actual shopping, which aggravated Mama to no end. "You know your Daddy didn't buy a single one of the gifts," she told us kids. We knew exactly what she meant.

The Christmas of 1963 was my most memorable. After opening our gifts on Christmas Eve, Daddy drove us around town to see the Christmas lights. Of course, we stopped by Pal's Drive-In.

When we arrived back home, Daddy hurriedly stepped up to the large front porch and looked in the big picture window. Mama quickly made her way up the steps, knowing Santa (my half brother) had delivered toys and clothes while we were gone.

"Look, Polly," Daddy said. "Do you see what I see?"

"Come quickly, Deb," Mama beckoned.

Danny peaked in the window and screamed, "Santa Claus came! Santa Claus came! Open the door, Daddy—hurry!"

As soon as Daddy unlocked the door, my gaze focused on the largest baby doll I had ever seen. Mama was tickled to introduce me to my new companion. "Look, Debbie! She'll walk with you and blink her eyes when you talk to her." Immediately, I burst into tears! Mama wanted to know whether I was excited or afraid of the doll, which was bigger than me. In truth, I was overwhelmed with emotion and from then on referred to her as "Betsy"—the sister I'd never had.

Although we did a lot of things together as a family when I was growing up, the fond memories began to fade during my teen years because Mama and Daddy constantly bickered and argued.

While Daddy was regularly trading and buying new cars, Mama was buying new curtains and bedspreads to redecorate the house. Not surprisingly, they never seemed to get ahead financially. This became an ongoing conflict. The strife only intensified as Daddy sought ways to make more money for his family.

---

"Every individual has a place to fill in the world and is important in some respect whether he chooses to be so or not."
*Nathaniel Hawthorn*

# Chapter 3

## Trouble On the Home Front

"Flowers grow out of dark moments."
*Corita Kent*

Daddy worked for W.J. Powell, a local produce company, when I was born. Before Danny started grade school, Daddy alternately took one of us with him on his route. I was thrilled when Danny started to school, for then I became first on the truck with Daddy.

We always left the house by 3:30 a.m. since his delivery stops took place prior to daylight. Although Daddy was thin and frail, he easily lifted the heavy crates filled with lettuce and cabbage and large forty-pound boxes of bananas.

After many years of employment with W.J. Powell Company, Daddy was terminated for taking home a box of bananas. He had expected the overripe bananas to be thrown away, so he didn't think it would be a problem. Obviously, Daddy was wrong. But the dismissal created an opportunity for Daddy to seek employment that offered better pay.

Uncle Charles, one of Mama's younger brothers, helped Daddy find a suitable job. Since he was employed by the Flint Beer Company, Uncle Charles secured a job for Daddy with the same company. There was only one downside—our family would have to move to Live Oak, Florida. In desperation, Daddy accepted the Florida position as a truck driver delivering beer to various liquor stores and convenience store chains.

Although we didn't want to leave in the middle of the school year, we knew we had no choice. As soon as we arrived in Live Oak, Mama went to the public schools to get us registered for classes.

In the evenings, Mama took us to the beer warehouse to help Daddy load his truck for the next day's deliveries. Before long, Danny and I were playing on the hundreds of cases of beer, jumping from one case to the other as if playing hopscotch. Finally, either Mama or Daddy would holler at the top of their lungs, "Y'all be quiet so we can think straight!"

In less than two months, Daddy realized that the move to Live Oak was not a good one. Mama urged him to find a job closer to home. Our Raleigh Avenue home was rented by Mama's cousin, so Mama knew we could easily move back.

Soon Daddy landed a job as a mobile home transporter with Parkwood Mobile Homes, headquartered in a town twenty-five miles away. He passed the required commercial driver's license exam with flying colors, and, in time, Daddy became one of the most valuable employees the company ever had.

The new job came with a significant pay increase. In fact, his first paycheck with Parkwood was over eight hundred dollars, which was a substantial amount of money in the late sixties. Since Daddy was making more money, I begged him to sell the Raleigh Avenue house and move to a more upscale neighborhood. But because he and Mama loved the home they had built, they chose to stay where their roots were so deeply planted.

Daddy's new job required transports all over the southeast. Each week he drove hundreds of miles, traveling from south Georgia and up the East Coast from daylight to sunset, as the law permitted.

His long absences from the family were a hardship for Mama and only added to their already strained relationship. Maintaining the household alone exhausted her, especially as we became teenagers.

Their biggest argument evolved around Daddy's sleep habits whenever he was home. Mama griped that he slept all the time. Daddy complained that he didn't sleep enough.

Instead of improving as a result of Daddy's pay increase, the discord only worsened. While Daddy loved making bigger paychecks and Mama loved the extra money, our family became even more dysfunctional.

While he always met his goal of making a good living, each of his jobs required odd work schedules—from rising early at the produce company to long hours of driving to deliver a mobile home—it seemed all roads led to insufficient rest and an overworked body. In addition, sitting for long periods in the cab of the truck created an unhealthy posture for Daddy's ailing back. Daddy turned to amphetamines in an effort to maintain the fast pace.

At least two weekends every month Mama and Daddy

took us to visit our aunt and uncle in Tallahassee. We loved playing with their three boys, our cousins.

Daddy also loved to drink beer on the weekends with our neighbors. When he and my uncle got together, he drank even more.

After those weekend shenanigans started, Mama adopted the motto: "When you can't beat them, join them." She and my aunt drank alongside Uncle Charles and Daddy, and before long they contributed to each others' drinking problems and marital woes.

After a full day of drinking with relatives, my parents herded us into the car for the drive back to Georgia, thirty-five miles away.

*How can we possibly get back home alive?* I often wondered. Sitting terrified in the backseat, I whispered prayers, frightened for my very life. My prayers lingered until we arrived safely home.

During those years, I often wished the state troopers would come along and pull Daddy and Mama over, but the troopers were never in the right place at the right time. Not only were my brothers and I concerned for our safety, but also for the safety of other innocent folks. My fears made me despise my parents' party life.

If my aunt and uncle came to our house, as they sometimes did, we experienced the same feelings of discomfort. Terry, the oldest of the three boys, and his brother, Chris, along with Danny and me developed our own mini support group. *How will my aunt and uncle and cousins get back to Tallahassee alive?* I wondered.

Shortly after Daddy arrived home late Friday evening, he and Mama started making plans for Saturday night. Their plans always included going to the dance, and the really big weekly decision was always the same: which nightclub in which neighboring town did they want to go that week? Drinking alongside my aunt and uncle, Mama and Daddy met several new couples at the dances. Soon their circle of drinking buddies tripled.

Mama loved to dance, but Daddy would never dance without a few beers first. He often started drinking early Saturday morning so that by the time they arrived at the dance he was more than ready to party.

I often asked, "Are you and Daddy going out tonight?" and always hoped Mama would answer with an emphatic no. For a long time that just didn't happen.

During those years, my only fond memory was of the loving times I shared with my friend, Lena, a caring elderly black lady who sat with us every Saturday evening. Over time, I grew to love and respect Lena. In fact, she became like a second mother to me. Lena in turn loved me and made me feel safe in my parents' absence. She cooked for us, cleaned, and ironed clothes, played games and anything else she could find to do on a Saturday night from about seven p.m. until the wee hours of the morning, when Mama and Daddy drove in as high as a kite.

Lena loved my parents. She recognized them as fine upstanding people, well respected, and hard working, but she realized, just as I did, they were allowing alcohol to rapidly take over their lives. She and I enjoyed many heart-to-heart talks about my parents' alcohol binges.

"Miss Lena, do you think Mama and Daddy will ever stop drinking?" I asked.

"Baby, the best thing we can do for them is to pray," she replied. And that we did.

"Miss Lena, will you please make me a cup of coffee?" I often requested.

I knew if Mama were home she wouldn't let me drink coffee "'cause it'll make you black." Lena laughed and joked with me, knowing the words had been said with utmost respect. "Add a dab of sugar with plenty of Carnation canned milk," I reminded her.

"Baby, I know what you like in your coffee." Of course she did. She had made me a cup many times before. It was our little secret.

I remember one Saturday evening Lena was ill and couldn't be there to care for us. Because we always felt secure with her, we weren't too happy with the thought of a new sitter. It was that night that we fell in love with Pauline, Lena's oldest daughter, who came to our rescue. We found it entertaining that Lena's daughter had the same name as Mama. Pauline became our second black mama.

A year or so later, Lena died suddenly from what the doctors told her family was a massive stroke. The shock was great for Danny, David, and me, the void even greater. But thankfully, we still had Pauline to lean on.

Sometimes Nancy spent Saturday nights at our house. As Mama got decked out for party night, Nancy fixed her hair and make-up. Daddy raved about Mama's pretty legs and her new hairdo. Mama usually shrugged off Daddy's compliments.

After they left to go to the dance, the boys played board games while Nancy and I played with paper dolls and the play kitchen in my bedroom.

Mama didn't handle alcohol as well as Daddy. The more beer he drank, the happier and more confident he became. But as Mama drank, her words and actions grew more careless and unpredictable. I learned to dread the weekly task of getting Mama into her gown and ready for bed.

Probably the most frightening episode of my life happened on a Sunday afternoon when Mama loaded us in the green Buick Skylark and headed to the Florida line to look for Daddy. Moments earlier she had seen him leave in a car with our neighbor, who was a known alcoholic. No doubt Mama knew exactly where they were headed—where everyone in our area headed on a Sunday—to the "line" to get more booze. (Florida law permits bottles sales on Sunday; Georgia still does not.) Since Mama had been drinking all day too, my brothers and I were scared out of our wits. We sat like zombies in the backseat of the car. Right there in the front seat next to Mama lay a loaded gun! That very day we expected one or both of our parents would die.

I also recall the overwhelming anxiety I felt during those early Sunday morning hours. My brothers and I were frequently awakened by Mama and Daddy's loud arguments, along with the noise from their knock-down, drag-out fights. Seared in my memory is the night Daddy broke Mama's finger after trying to grab the scissors from her hand as she tried to injure him.

In addition to being heavy weekend drinkers, Mama and Daddy were heavy smokers. Their smoking added to my anxiety when they came home drunk. Many nights I stayed awake to make sure they didn't burn the house down with a dropped cigarette. Only after they were in the bed for the night could I comfortably close my sleepy brown eyes.

Daddy had worked for Parkwood Mobile Homes

for seven years when the economy deteriorated and the upper end of the mobile home industry followed. At the age of forty-five, Daddy was forced to start all over again.

He landed a similar position with Liberty Homes located in the industrial park not far from our home. Mama and Daddy felt this was a positive change. No longer would he have to drive the long distance every Monday morning.

With the job change his drinking slowed for a while, but it wasn't long before he returned home from long trips smelling like a brewery.

One evening Mama received a phone call from Daddy. It frightened us to hear him say, "I've just been held up by a man who has a dog with big, shiny white teeth!" This hallucination was caused by a combination of alcohol and stimulants.

Daddy eventually lost his driver's licenses and his transport job due to the alcohol addiction. Fortunately, the company offered him a job as the plant security guard. Once Daddy was off the road, he stopped using the stimulants. Staying awake was no longer important.

But his endless search for more money and a better life and Mama's ongoing discontentment began to eat at the fabric of their relationships.

I repeatedly heard Mama say she and Daddy stayed together for the kids' sake—that is, until the strife caused them to divorce when little brother reached age sixteen.

---

"God is our refuge and strength, an
ever-present help in trouble."
*Psalm 46:1*

# Chapter 4

## Safe on the Farm

"Things turn out best for the people who
make the best of the way things turn out."
*H. Jackson Brown, Jr.*

My relatives and I referred to it as Furney Farm, located outside the tiny town of Pavo, Georgia. I enjoyed spending summers with Uncle Dick and my mother's sister, Aunt Wilma, on their sixty-one-acre country estate.

I was six when their only son, Don, was killed while driving home from college for the Thanksgiving holiday. Aunt Wilma and Uncle Dick had a terrible time dealing with the loss, but their loneliness lessened a bit with the arrival of nieces and nephews who visited often. Although several family members accused me of being their favorite niece, I believe they simply responded to my love for them.

Chickens, hogs, and cows occupied the farm, so Aunt Wilma and Uncle Dick worked hard and stayed busy caring for the animals. I watched Uncle Dick milk the cows and observed as Aunt Wilma made butter. She was an excellent cook and always prepared three meals a day. At the same time, she taught me the proper way to set a table and fold a napkin. I learned to make her special apple tarts using Aunt Wilma's own recipe—probably the one handed down from Grandma. It was there at the farm that I learned to value giving thanks before meals.

Relatives or friends could stop by Furney Farm anytime and find food enough to feed an army. After Grandma died in the late eighties, all family reunions took place at Furney Farm.

Although I learned a lot about the farm animals during my summer vacations, I gained even greater benefits. I learned the importance of church attendance and studying God's Word, and I always looked forward to Vacation Bible School at their little country church. Aunt Wilma taught Sunday school and was a VBS leader. Uncle Dick served as a deacon. Anytime I was with them, we attended all the church services.

My occasional visits to Furney Farm also provided a short respite from the strife at home. Because Aunt Wilma and Uncle Dick did not permit alcohol consumption on their farm, I felt safe knowing my stay would be peaceful.

During those years, both my aunt and uncle were active members of Pavo Baptist Church. I admired their dedication and loyalty to the church as well as their relationship with each other. They taught me through example the importance of spiritual health.

It was early Sunday morning, August 13, 1967, at the young age of eleven, that I sat in the living room of our Raleigh Avenue home listening to Billy Graham on television. When he issued the invitation, and while the crowd sang, 'Just As I Am', I saw my need of forgiveness and accepted Jesus Christ as my Lord and Savior. A few weeks later, I was baptized by the pastor of a small Baptist church adjacent to the elementary school. I always believed God had an important purpose for my life. The very first Scripture I remember memorizing is Philippians 4:11(KJV): "Not that I speak in respect of want, for I have learned in whatever state I am, in this to be content." I've reminded myself of that vital message many times.

When I was four years old, my parents took Danny and me to a small independent Baptist church in town. Our faithful family of four sat on the left side of the church in the next-to-the-last pew.

One Sunday morning, Danny and I discovered a songbook propped in the rack on the back of the pew. We started giggling when we noticed a perfectly round hole the size of a nickel extending completely through the book, as if it had been drilled. And try as we might, we couldn't stop laughing. When Daddy gave us the eye a few minutes later, we knew without a doubt that we were in big trouble.

After that incident, they never took us to church again; they were much too embarrassed. I only learned years later that Mama and Daddy were close to making a decision for Christ. Their plan was to join East Side Baptist Church.

Not surprisingly, I grew up feeling somewhat responsible for my parents' failure to return to church. When I specifically asked the Lord to show me what I could do, He told me to reflect the love of Christ by my quiet and reverent example.

### Special Memories of My Grandparents

Since we rarely visited Daddy's side of the family, my maternal grandparents were the only Grandma and Grandpa I really knew. Grandma dipped snuff, played the piano, crocheted beautiful blankets, and whipped any opponent at checkers. Grandpa chewed tobacco, worked hard on their farm, and ran his country store in the Salem community.

Each year Mama and Daddy took an adult vacation, leaving us with Grandma and Grandpa. I remember one specific incident that happened while staying with them in Coolidge.

One afternoon, Uncle Doyle, one of their seven sons, came to visit. After a time, I decided Grandma and my uncle had spent enough time socializing. Because I was ready for her to play with me, I traipsed in and out the front door, each time slamming the screen door.

"Don't slam that screen door again, *little lady,* because if you do I'm going to wear your fanny out," she warned me.

My strong will surfaced as I made one last trip through the front door, slamming it even harder that time. True to her word, Grandma used her flyswatter and whipped my little fanny, just as she'd cautioned me. From that day forward, my respect for her increased immensely.

Since Grandpa died when I was just ten, I don't have as many precious memories of him as I do Grandma.

In later years, after Grandpa's death, Grandma moved from the farm to the housing projects located halfway between our house and London Bridge. Anytime we rode our bikes to Taylor's Store, Danny and I made sure we stopped by to check on her. Shortly after I graduated from Thomas Area Technical School, now known as Southwest Georgia Technical College, Grandma's health failed, and she moved to Sunrise Nursing Home in Moultrie, where she lived comfortably for eleven more years.

My very first experience as a newly licensed nurse began with my participation as a caregiver for Grandma. Later, my visits to the nursing home only added to my interest in geriatric nursing—especially since I witnessed firsthand how much Grandma enjoyed living there until her death at the "young" age of ninety–three.

---

"The past cannot be regained, although we can learn from it; the future is not yet ours even though we must plan for it . . . Time is now. We have only today."

*Charles Hummell*

# Chapter 5

## Shy Girl … With a Vision

"No one can make you feel
inferior without your consent."
*Eleanor Roosevelt*

I struggled with physical imperfections that haunted me from the second grade through my first year of college, particularly the horrible Coke bottle glasses that I wore. I couldn't see without them, so I had no choice but to wear them. Each time I looked in the mirror, I felt a fresh stab of embarrassment.

Because I was the only four-eyed second-grader in my classroom at Harper School, my schoolmates often made fun of me. In the third grade, there was one boy who wore glasses, but his were nowhere near as thick as mine. Although he and I became friends, it still didn't help my feelings knowing I was the only girl with glasses in my classroom.

Then there was that wide space between my two front teeth. I was certain that the gap stood out like a sore thumb. Though people admired my dimples, I still couldn't forget that glaring space. My dentist recommended braces when I was twelve, but the lack of finances made it impossible. It wasn't until I graduated from college and started to work full time that I could finally afford to have the space between my teeth corrected. That correction made all the difference in the world for my self-esteem.

My fair complexion also set me apart from others during the days when as a teenager it was cool to bake in the sun to acquire a tan. Well, because I, too, wanted a tan, I lay in the sun with several of my friends and basked in its rays. Within thirty minutes I had blistered. Less than a week later, my skin started to peel. I was left with not only my usual fair complexion, but the addition of more than my fair share of freckles. Meanwhile, my friends had begun the process of developing their beautiful tans that day, which they carried all summer long. No matter how much I wanted or how hard I tried, I simply never felt like I fit in.

My brothers constantly teased me, calling my skinny legs "bird legs." Anytime I donned a skirt or pair of shorts, my oldest brother would ask, "Is that a string hanging from your skirt?" Then he would chuckle. "Oh, no ... My mistake. It's not a string. It's your leg!" In my defense, Daddy told the boys my legs were pretty—just like Mama's. And even though their playful words were said in jest, it was difficult for me to overcome the pain I felt.

I was never truly overweight, but I did add a few excess pounds when I reached puberty—just one more reason for my brothers to tease me. They called me "Chubby," a name that made me feel even more self-conscious.

My second grade teacher evidently saw something in me I couldn't see in myself when she chose me to portray the female lead in our school play, *Beauty and the Beast.* While that role improved my feelings of self-worth, I remember just as vividly an incident in the eighth grade that destroyed all the worth Beauty had engendered.

Six girls, including me, auditioned to become part of the junior varsity drill team. The judges planned to announce the winners at 2:45 p.m. the following afternoon—just moments before the school day ended. I took for granted that I'd be wearing one of those cute red and gold drill team uniforms.

All of us contestants sat on the bleachers anxiously awaiting the announcement of the winners. The judges asked the winners to report to the center of the athletic field when our names were called. I had no idea five girls were to be selected. To my horror, I sat alone when the exercise ended.

It took all the courage I could muster to sit through the remaining five minutes of the school day. I could hardly contain my feeling of shame and embarrassment, which by this time had settled like a huge lump in my throat.

The minute that school bell rang I jumped off the bleacher and raced to the car as fast as I could. Never was I so relieved to see Mama parked there, waiting for me. Occasionally, she would be five or ten minutes late picking me up, but thankfully she was on time that day. The minute I slipped inside the car, Mama sensed something was wrong. I couldn't hold that awful sting of failure another second. I burst into tears!

Sharing my painful disappointment, Mama tried to console me. "Don't worry about it, honey. You couldn't be in both the school band and on the drill team anyway. Don't let it get you down—just keep playing your coronet."

In the third grade, I begged Mama to let me transfer from Harper School to East Side Elementary. Danny stayed at Harper, but I was determined to make the transfer. Within a few weeks after the move, I realized I had made a terrible mistake. Most of the kids who attended East Side lived in the country club area, and it didn't take long to realize I didn't fit with the high-society bunch. Living on Raleigh Avenue and formerly attending Harper School provided more than sufficient evidence to my peers that my family was not affluent. I was very uncomfortable at East Side.

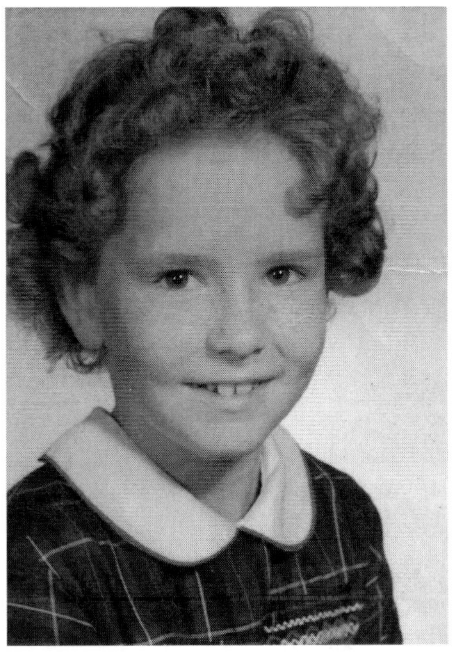

*Third-grader at East Side. Freckle-faced and too embarrassed to have my picture taken with my glasses. I had a scar over my right eye.*

Because Mama and Daddy had always taught me to complete a task no matter how tough, I knew before asking that there would be no transfer back to Harper. Not in the middle of the school year.

"You made the decision to go to East Side," said Mama. "You can return to Harper next year." As hard as it was, I stuck it out. Persevering in difficult circumstances became deeply ingrained in my character.

Every morning a circle of elite third-graders gathered under the large oak tree on the east side of the campus. Because I felt like everyone was staring at me as I got out of the car and walked toward the group, I took to subterfuge: slipping into the circle between one or two girls in hopes that no one would recognize my presence.

Recess and lunch periods were rarely fun. I wasn't sure what to say to my uppity peers. I was incredibly relieved when my third grade year at East Side Elementary finally ended.

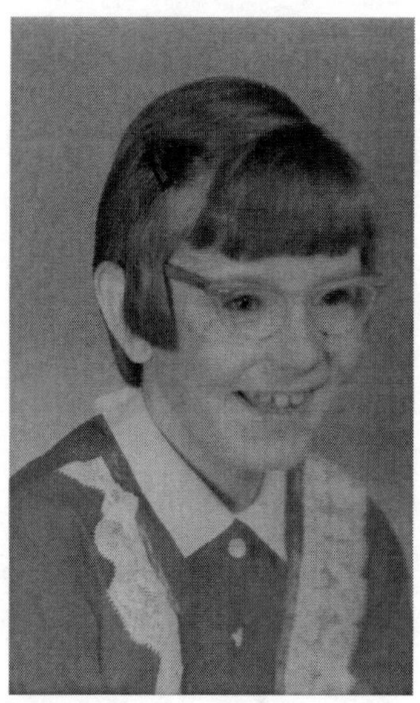

*A four-eyed fifth-grader back at Harper School.*

In junior high, it seemed all the girls had boyfriends while I hung out with my girlfriends, quietly attending class and studying hard, always excelling in the classroom.

One day a guy who had a crush on me called me on the phone. Mama listened in on our conversation and immediately demanded I hang up. From then on, every time I saw him in the corridor at school, I felt a renewed sense of embarrassment. I was never allowed to date or talk to boys, not even on the phone, until I was sixteen.

With Daddy gone on the road most of my teenage years, it was up to Mama to make all the decisions. My brothers and I learned quickly not to question her authority.

When I was fourteen, I was offered a job at the local Dairy Queen. I was happy with my first job making $1.25 per hour. Sometimes I got nervous when customers arrived at the counter, and it almost felt like I was standing before an audience each time I asked, "May I help you, please?"

*Fourteen years old with thick glasses and freckles multiplied from basking in the sun.*

Nancy worked at the Zesto Drive-In located on Madison Street, so when her employer asked if she knew anyone interested in working, she quickly mentioned my name. "We could work together," she said. "Besides, it's closer to Raleigh Avenue and less distance to drive."

I loved working at Dairy Queen, and with my work ethic, only a good reason such as higher pay or better benefits would allow me to change jobs. Mama and Daddy often preached: "Job-hopping is not an option. Find a job and stick with it."

Nancy kept encouraging me until finally I talked with Mr. Kat, who offered me ten cents more per hour. "It's a promotion," Daddy said. "You'll be making more money."

His approval was reason enough. "I'll take the job, Mr. Kat. When do I start?"

By the time I was sixteen, I had bought my first vehicle, a 1970 yellow Maverick. I liked paying my own monthly payments of $64.46. After two years it was the first tangible item I could truly say was mine.

As a young teenager, I remember my brother's fiancée was hospitalized with a urinary tract infection. While I was visiting, I was intrigued by her catheter bag. When the nurse came to empty it, I asked if I could watch her. "It's up to the patient," she answered.

"Can I watch, please?"

"Of course you can," she answered.

Later, I added, "At home my brothers let me bandage their scrapes, Mama lets me rub lotion on her feet and legs, and Daddy wants me to massage his back. When I grow up I want to be a nurse, too."

Since that eighth grade experience as a failed performer, I never again felt accepted. In fact, the fear of rejection limited my willingness to stick my neck out. With that in mind, I begged Mama to let me finish my last year of high school at the technical school. The school was smaller and would be more comfortable, especially since I already knew the direction my career path would take.

Since Mama's boss worked at the tech school, I didn't have a problem convincing her that going to Tech my senior year was a good thing. Besides, Mama knew my desire was to become a nurse. I was ecstatic when the technical school approved my application.

However, the cost of tuition was an issue. Since Tech offered a specialized curricula, students had to pay tuition. I knew Mama and Daddy would not pay the expenses, so I confronted the challenge on my own. Working part time, first at Dairy Queen and then at the Zesto, provided me the chance to start saving. I was bound and determined to become a Licensed Practical Nurse… and not even a lack of funds would stand in the way of my success.

---

"For God did not give us a spirit of timidity, but a spirit of power, of love and of self-discipline."
*2 Timothy 1:7*

# Chapter 6

## I Am Someone Special!

"Forget past mistakes. Forget failures. Forget everything except what you're going to do now and do it."
*William Durant*

As soon as the school bell rang at 3:15 p.m., I left the science lab and hurriedly made my way to my bright yellow Maverick. Because I was scheduled to work at the Zesto, I rushed home to change clothes in preparation for my shift.

When I arrived at the fast food diner, my boss, Mr. Kat, flipped the door lock open for me to enter and kindly greeted me. Just as I punched the time clock, I heard a man's voice. While donning my burgundy smock, I caught a glimpse of a handsome young man standing at the counter.

The distinct sound of his voice prompted me to look again. He had blond hair and wire-framed glasses and a big smile that displayed perfectly straight teeth. His penetrating look assured me he could accomplish anything he set out to do. But even more interesting, he seemed like a happy-go-lucky person. Mr. Kat accepted payment for a banana split and invited him to come again. Not giving any further thought to the moment, I washed my hands, preparing for my five-hour shift.

Anytime Mr. Kat asked for a counter girl to work overtime, I eagerly welcomed the opportunity. My plans of entering the upcoming practical nursing class at the technical school motivated me to save every dime I could make. It was my responsibility to pay the costs of nursing school in lieu of attending my senior year of high school. My junior year was half over. I had only a few months left to earn the money for tuition and expenses.

That particular day, Nancy was also scheduled to work from five till closing. As soon as she arrived, Mr. Kat said good-bye, leaving us fully in charge of the Zesto. As best friends, she and I worked well together. We relished the not-so-busy moments, allowing time for girl talk.

"Oh, by the way, Nancy, have you seen a young blond-haired guy come by here before?" I asked. "He's about five foot six, I'd say. He's got a real pretty smile."

"I bet you're talking about the newspaper guy—the one who always gets a large cherry slush," she answered.

"Uh … no, he ordered a banana split today," I replied.

"Oh yeah, some days he does get a banana split. I forgot about that. Does he usually come about the time we come to work?" she asked. "Like maybe around four?"

"That's the time he was here this afternoon."

"Oh yeah, I've seen him several times. I think he comes by just about everyday. He's really a nice guy from what I can tell."

"I think he's really cute," I admitted.

"Hey, why don't you flirt with him a little? Let him know what you think. At least let him know you like him."

"Me, flirt? Just how comical is that?" I giggled at the very idea. "He probably wouldn't like me. Not with my Coke bottle glasses and freckles. But at least he wouldn't see my skinny legs behind the counter."

"Well, now wait a minute. You know he wears glasses too," she reminded me. "Don't be so doggone hard on yourself. I think he's probably a couple of years older than you—which is okay. Hey, why don't you ask Danny about him?"

"Oh yeah, that's a great idea. I hadn't even thought of that. Since they both work for the newspaper company, I could definitely get the inside scoop from my brother." After a pause, I added, "You know what, Nancy? I bet he already has a girlfriend."

Because the rest of the evening was busy, we had little idle time to talk, but I continued to remember how the young man had looked standing at the counter. *What a neat guy. I am certainly going to find out more about him.*

Later on that evening, just before closing time, Nancy swept and mopped the floor on the kitchen side of the restaurant. I cleaned the front side, including the milkshake mixer, and wiped down all the counters.

In the quietness of the small room, my thoughts raced back to my ugly, thick glasses. *I doubt seriously he'll be the least bit interested in me.*

By 9:15 p.m., Nancy and I had finished our cleaning chores. As we started to leave the diner, I quickly locked the front door. "See you tomorrow, girl," I said.

"Don't forget to ask Danny about, uh ... Blondie," she reminded me as we both got in our cars and headed to our homes.

I could hardly wait to get home to talk to Danny, asking him no less than a hundred questions. "Tell me about that blond-haired guy, the one who drives the newspaper van," I said.

"Oh, you must be talking about Mickey. He's a great guy. He's our route supervisor at the office. He graduated from Central High School and lives in Boston, I think," he said. "He's dating some girl that lives over in Boston, but I don't think it's too serious. Actually, he mentioned seeing you recently at the Zesto. He was surprised when I told him you were my sister."

"I figured he already had a girlfriend."

"I wouldn't count on that," Danny commented. "He told me you were really cute. You ought to talk to him the next time he stops by the Zesto. You never can tell. I know he likes that cherry slush y'all have up there."

"He also likes banana splits," I confirmed.

A month or so later, out of the blue Mr. Kat told me, "Debbie, some guy with glasses came by yesterday and asked if you were here. I've been noticing that he comes nearly the same time everyday. I think he's sweet on you!"

"Are you kidding me, Mr. Kat?" I asked, feeling skeptical.

"No. He asked specifically for you. Isn't your name Debbie?" he joked.

"Well, yeah…" The incredible thought of Mickey coming to see me at the Zesto was more than my timid mind could comprehend. For the first time in my life, I was ecstatic merely thinking about the remote possibility. It was hard for me to focus on work the rest of the day.

Mickey began stopping by the Zesto every day; some days I was working, and other days I wasn't. He never failed to question the counter ladies on duty: "When does Debbie work again?"

They always told me, "That newspaper guy came by yesterday and said to tell you hello." By then my imagination was having a field day.

The restaurant had no seating area, so our visits lasted only as long as it took for me to prepare his cherry slush or banana split, ring up the sale, and politely hand him his change.

I had no idea that Mickey himself was also shy. Three months passed before the opportunity finally came to get to know him. One Friday evening he called me at home. "Would you like to ride with me to Tallahassee to deliver a load of newspapers?"

"I'd love to go."

"I'll pick you up in about an hour."

*Just the two of us*, I kept thinking while waiting for him to arrive. My heart pounded as I anticipated our first date.

We enjoyed a wonderful trip, and following the delivery, we stopped at Whataburger on Thomasville Road and enjoyed our first meal together. Away from other people, we relaxed enough to talk.

From that night on, the two of us were inseparable. Mickey spent many evenings at our house, where my parents treated him like a son. It wasn't long before he took me to meet his parents. I was thrilled when his family welcomed me with open arms.

While working at the Zesto, I met a nice gentleman, the proprietor of King Record Shop, which was located across the street. Once he got to know me, Mr. Len tried his best to hire me as manager of his record store. After declining his offer, I suggested he consider employing my mother.

Mama became his store manager while I doggedly pursued my dream of becoming a nurse.

In the summer of 1974, shortly before my senior year, I was presented with a new job opportunity along with another pay hike. The fine owners of Maryland Fried Chicken offered me a forty-five-cents-an-hour increase. I needed all the money I could earn to pay my tuition before the deadline.

"I plan to take classes at the technical school in the fall," I said during the interview with my new bosses. "Will it be okay if I study at night while on the job as long as I'm not busy and I get my work done?"

"Of course, it'll be just fine. Just make sure you complete all your chores before closing up each night."

The flexibility to study made it the perfect job for me during the time I was in LPN school.

Soon Mickey began to appear at the restaurant shortly before closing time. He always mopped the floors before escorting me to my car.

Working together on a daily basis, Danny and Mickey became very good friends. Mickey and I double-dated with Danny and Debbie Rehberg, his soon-to-be-wife, and the four of us became close. (Since both Danny's wife and I had the same given name, she agreed to be called by her last name. In the many years she's been a part of our family, she continues to be known as Rehberg.)

Mickey and I worked hard to make our own way. The two of us enjoyed the same hobbies, especially bowling and going to movies at Gateway Theater. There is no other way to say it—we were falling in love!

Both of us were Christians. Although we didn't go to church every time the doors were opened, Summerhill

Baptist became our home church. It wasn't long before I learned that Mickey was a very generous person. Every other Friday, when he got paid, he treated his parents, his younger sister, and me to a buffet lunch at the Holiday Inn.

On Valentine's Day in 1975, the halfway mark of my senior year, Mickey surprised me with a pre-engagement ring. This was a popular "first step" for young lovers in the mid-seventies. Although I was a nail-biter, I soon gave up that nasty habit. I wanted my hands to look pretty to show off my ring.

*Mickey and I at the Junior–Senior prom, 1975*

April 11, 1975, was a memorable day for two reasons: Mickey and I were privileged to serve as attendants at Danny and Rehberg's wedding, while earlier that day I was blessed to be named winner of the 1975 Georgia Occupational Award of Leadership. I received several gift certificates from area businesses as well as five shares of Flowers Baking Company stock.

Mr. Paul Sewell, school administrator, proudly presented the award to me at the Friday Kiwanis Club luncheon meeting. I cherished his words of admiration written in a special card he gave me: *Congratulations, Debbie. May this be just a beginning!*

Along with Mickey's love for me, I won the highest award at the technical school. Then, for the first time, I began to realize ... perhaps *I am* someone special! Because of my shy nature, I always struggled when called upon to speak in public. Even after winning the award, I was never completely comfortable with the spotlight.

I received my high school diploma, and only three months later, I completed requirements for my nursing diploma. At eighteen, I had already fulfilled the Georgia requirements to successfully function as an LPN.

One week after graduation, I proudly accepted my first nursing position at Archbold Memorial Hospital. I worked on Two West, an orthopedic unit. Most of my patients were elderly; many had suffered a fractured hip or some other broken bone.

Although I was passionate about nursing, Mickey wasn't yet sure of his career choice. He loved his work with the newspaper, but he wanted to find something he could pursue as a lifelong career. "Debbie, it's obvious you know what you want to do, and you're happy doing it," he said. "I think you must be Thomasville's Florence Nightingale." I was thrilled knowing he thought so highly of me.

Two months later, Mickey enrolled in the Emergency Medical Technician class at the tech school. By the end of that year, he was certified. Together we hoped to alleviate suffering through the helping professions.

On Christmas Eve that year, Mickey gave me an engagement ring, and together we decided to be married on May 21, 1976. By then we were sure we'd be well established in our careers. As always, I was adamant in that I wanted everything planned and paid in full *before* we were married.

Shortly after the New Year, I encountered major and unexpected vision problems. On a Friday afternoon, while working at the hospital, I started seeing black spots. Soon Dr. Blackman shared with Mickey and my parents the diagnosis: retinal tears in both eyes. "Without emergency intervention," he said, "the tears can rapidly lead to detachment and subsequent blindness." Within seventy-two hours, Dr. Bridges, an ophthalmologist, performed my first eye surgery. Three times in three consecutive months—January, February, and March of 1976—he operated to seal the numerous tears, which most likely had resulted from severe nearsightedness generated from when I contracted German measles as a child.

As I lay hospitalized on Valentine's Day, with both eyes completely bandaged, Mickey came in with the local newspaper. He was anxious to read a special one-by-two-inch classified ad to me: *To the Sweetest Girl in the Whole Wide World.* Those words had been placed in the middle of a heart-shaped ad. That was all it took to convince me that Mickey was the man God had for me.

Because of the eye operations, we decided to move our wedding date back two months. "Unless something drastic happens, we will be married on July 23," I told Mickey and my coworkers.

A month before the wedding day, Mickey surprised me with a written note left on the windshield of my car at the hospital: *I love you more than you will ever know. I love you so much that I wish we would get married tonight!" Love, MM—your husband-to-be.*

Without a doubt, I knew I was blessed with the most

wonderful man in the world, and I was finally convinced—*I really am someone special because he loves me!*

---

"For I know the plans I have for you," declares the Lord, "plans to prosper you and not to harm you, plans to give you hope and a future."
*Jeremiah 29:11*

# Chapter 7

## Wedding Plans in the Air

"Love is patient, love is kind. It does not envy, it does not boast, it is not proud. It is not rude, it is not self-seeking, it is not easily angered, it keeps no record of wrongs. Love does not delight in evil but rejoices with the truth. It always protects, always trusts, always hopes, always perseveres. Love never fails."
*1 Corinthians 13:4–8a*

A beautiful sixteen-by-twenty wedding picture of a friend hung in the foyer at Gateway Cinema Theater. Each time my fiancé, Mickey, and I went to the movies it caught our eye. We admired many of Miss Sara's award-winning photos. We agreed that she was the photographer we wanted to take our wedding pictures. In a short time, we had saved enough that I was able to write the check, well in advance, for $188.31 to Sara's Studio to photograph our wedding, to be held July 23, 1976.

As part of Miss Sara's commitment, she also shot several engagement photos for us. Browsing through the negatives, Mickey selected one particular favorite. "I wish

I'd asked Miss Sara to make me a five-by-seven," he said. "I'd place it in the glove compartment of my car. Then I'd have it with me at all times."

Although I wanted a photo of the two of us in the engagement announcement, Mickey preferred to display my photo alone. In the end, the photo of his choice was placed in the local *Times Enterprise*.

I surprised Mickey on his twenty-third birthday with an exquisitely wrapped package. I had hidden something special in gradually larger boxes, all of which he had to unwrap before finding his gift. Finally, he saw it—the framed five-by-seven engagement picture. He beamed at the thought of sharing it with his ambulance partners.

His EMT buddies always flattered me with heartfelt compliments, like the time Dennis said, "Mickey really loves you, Debbie. I hope you know that."

Forrest said, "He loves that picture showing your dimples. Did you know he keeps it in his car?"

While working at the hospital, I often observed the gorgeous floral baskets sent to my patients from Singletary's Flower Shop. Mickey and I mutually agreed that our wedding flowers would be absolutely perfect if Mr. Jimmy (Singletary) handled the arrangements.

I chose pink carnations for my bridesmaids' bouquets. Mr. Jimmy and I decided the pink would emphasize the floor-length bridesmaid gowns of dotted Swiss. He suggested accenting the attendants' white ripple brim hats with a dab of greenery and several long streamers of pink satin ribbon. Two months before the wedding date, Mickey and I were excited when we hand delivered the final payment of $180.77 to Mr. Jimmy.

Since the photographer and the florist were our

largest wedding expenses, we were thrilled to have those heavy burdens behind us.

Mickey specifically ordered the men's tuxes and paid for them in late spring. His wedding attire consisted of black slacks, a pink ruffled shirt, and a white jacket. The best man and his attendants would be dressed exactly the same except their jackets were black.

I stashed away twenty-five dollars in an envelope every payday for well over a month. When I had the required amount, I wrote the preacher's name on the envelope. Mickey's pastor, Reverend Harold Pullen, had agreed to marry us at the small historic Summerhill Baptist Church.

Mickey and I labored intensely over the selection of the perfect wedding cake to grace the reception table. We pinched pennies and worked hard to make our money go as far as possible. We were delighted when his friend's mom offered to make the cake as a wedding gift.

The pink reception napkins imprinted with our names and the wedding date were perfect.

Because our hospital friends were eager to share our special day, we ended up adding fifty invitations to the original order of 125.

I remember how excited I was the afternoon I found a size two petite wedding dress for sale in the classified section of the local newspaper. I quickly dialed the phone number and asked the lady if I could come and see the dress—right then.

Mickey and I were astonished at her willingness to sell the dress for only fifty dollars, a fraction of the cost of a new dress. Worn only once, it looked brand new. I immediately fell in love with it.

Because finances were tight, we decided to sell

my five shares of Flowers Banking Company stock to cover the price of the gown.

The last week in April, Mickey received confirmation in the mail reserving a room on the night of July 23 at the Holiday Inn in Valdosta, Georgia. That very same week he submitted the final payment for a three-night honeymoon reservation for July 24–27 at the Holiday Inn in Orlando. Though we had discussed spending our honeymoon at Disney World, he was so excited that he secretly made the plans and paid for them in full without telling me. As the time drew nearer, I asked, "What about the Disney World tickets?"

"It's all been taken care of," he assured me.

Time passed slowly as we waited impatiently for the big day.

"I plan to put one hundred dollars aside from my next two paychecks so we'll have extra spending money on our honeymoon," Mickey told me. I agreed that was a terrific idea.

The month before the wedding was a busy one with several bridal showers held by friends as well as the ladies from Summerhill Baptist Church. Mickey and I enjoyed writing the thank-you notes together.

In early January, following our Christmas engagement, Mickey had been offered an option to buy a house from Mr. Aspinwall, his long-time friend and owner of the hardware store in the little town of Boston.

Our combined incomes could comfortably handle the twelve thousand-dollar mortgage. Together we went to look at the house. We did not want to make any long-term plans without considering each other's opinions.

Because it was a great investment and would make

a wonderful home, Mickey purchased the charming cottage located on Old Boston Road, eight miles east of Thomasville. Once it was ours, we worked hard together to make the necessary repairs. We always paid cash for the materials.

Our new little house was perfect. The small two-bedroom yellow frame cottage, surrounded by an acre of land, had a spacious living room, dining room, kitchen, and bathroom. Both bedrooms were roomy and had a walk-in closet separating them. The house had ten-foot ceilings and many tall windows, as well as French doors that divided the dining and living rooms. The inside of the house was fully carpeted with paneled walls. In the kitchen was a convenient center bar with a custom-built cabinet base. The bathroom had an avocado green tub and sink with custom-made white cabinets.

A month before the wedding, our home was completely furnished—right down to soap in the soap dish, food in the kitchen cabinets, and twin wooden rocking chairs, one for each of us. When Mickey and I found a special sale, we stocked up on the item, like a dozen or so rolls of paper towels for the kitchen or ten cans of cleanser.

Because we were on a budget, we paid cash for the inside furnishings. Mickey cherished his walnut bedroom suite—a family heirloom from his grandmother. My grandparents sold us a washer and dryer for two hundred dollars. We purchased a beautiful cane-back occasional chair from my oldest brother for thirty-five dollars and later an avocado green recliner from the Woolworth store for thirty-nine dollars. From hand-me-down furniture to store bargains to yard sales, we were determined to have our home ready to occupy when we returned from our honeymoon.

In early March, Mickey and I agonized over the decision to purchase an additional tract of land located between our home and the house next door. After careful consideration, we decided the land would add to our investment. I wrote a check for its purchase.

Two months later, in early May, he and I struggled with another decision: whether or not to have white vinyl siding installed on the outside of our house. We opted for the siding, believing it would eliminate future exterior maintenance problems.

We painted the outside window trim jet black and added shutters to the windows. Then we used razor blades to scrape the old paint off the floor-length windows. A large rocking chair porch encompassed the entire length of the house.

*The "perfect" house for the perfect couple.*

Mickey's favorite phrase was: "It's the perfect house for the perfect couple."

Invitations for my July eighth lingerie shower were in the mail. My friends, who were hosting the shower, teased me often as they finalized the plans. When they made sexy comments trying to embarrass me, I shocked them with snappy replies. We were all excited to see the silky, frilly gowns and undergarments I'd receive at the shower.

"It won't matter what it looks like," I teased right back. "I won't need any of them anyway—after all, it'll be our wedding night!"

"Did shy little Debbie say that?" They giggled.

With less than three weeks left, only the last minute business details remained. We opened a joint checking account at the Citizens & Southern Bank. A branch was also located in Boston, allowing us the flexibility of using either one. Checks were ordered in our soon-to-be married name.

Mickey had the telephone installed on Thursday afternoon, July first.

On Saturday afternoon, the third of July, he and I hung a freshly painted swing on our big front porch. Daddy promised to help Mickey install a chandelier in the dining room the next evening. Other than that, neither of us could think of a thing left to do. We were two very excited lovebirds!

"We can sit back and relax now while we wait for our big day," Mickey said. "It's not going to be long now. I love you, Debbie."

"I love you too, Mickey."

---

"In dreams and in love there are no impossibilities."
*Janos Arnay*

# Chapter 8

## A Life-Changing Phone Call

"And we know that in all things God works
for the good of those who love Him, who have
been called according to His purpose."
*Romans 8:28*

Working as a hospital nurse on Two West provided its own unique challenges. The holidays always seemed to bring in more business because there were more falls and accidents and less nursing staff to handle the incoming admissions. Not only did that Fourth of July fall on a weekend, but it was also a full moon.

July 4, 1976, was an unusually stressful and busy day for me as I fulfilled my duties as a Licensed Practical Nurse. Making beds and helping my patients bathe and dress were the order of the day during my morning shift: 6:45 a.m. to 3:15 p.m.

One female patient understood my delay in assisting with her usual morning care. After learning she was a Registered Nurse and a pastor's wife, we connected immediately. A kind, attractive lady in her late thirties, she asked if I would shave her legs. She had undergone back surgery, and her physician's orders limited her to standing or lying flat in bed. While she lay in bed, I shaved her legs, which gave us time to visit.

Making conversation, I said, "I'm getting married in nineteen days."

"And who is the lucky groom?" she asked.

"Oh, his name is Mickey McLendon," I answered excitedly.

"Where does he work?"

"He works for the county as an EMT."

"So you both work in the medical field?"

"Yes, ma'am, we enjoy helping others."

"Did you meet Mickey while working at the hospital?"

"No, ma'am. We met through my older brother, Danny."

"Did Mickey always want to be an EMT?"

"I'm not sure he really knew what he wanted to do until I persuaded him to enroll in EMT training. I spent many nights helping him study to achieve his certification, and it seems he's found his niche there. I'm really proud of him. The pay and benefits are good with the county, which is good, because we are planning to have three children."

"How long have y'all been dating?"

"About two and a half years."

"Where are y'all going on your honeymoon?"

"To Disney World. I haven't been there since I was a little girl, and I'm really looking forward to it. We've already paid for our trip."

"Will y'all live in Thomasville?"

"Oh, I wish you could see our cute little house between Thomasville and Boston. It's the perfect size for us—all furnished too. We're trying hard to have everything paid for before we get married—except the house itself, of course."

"Did Mickey work today too?"

"No, ma'am, he's off, but he's coming to eat lunch with me. And this afternoon we plan to finish writing thank-you notes. We've already had three bridal showers."

"Oh, that'll be fun. Sounds like y'all have it all together."

"Oh, yes, ma'am. We're more than ready for our big day."

I had finished the task. "Is that better? See what you think."

"Thanks so much, Debbie, for taking the extra time with me. I appreciate this more than you'll ever know. I'll be praying for you and Mickey to have a wonderful life together."

Suddenly, I realized it was 12:30 p.m.—time for my lunch break. I was sure Mickey was standing at the front entrance waiting for me. I eagerly took the stairs down to the cafeteria of the three-story building, but after a quick search, I realized Mickey was nowhere to be found. I proceeded through the cafeteria line, expecting him to come rushing in at any moment. At the register I looked around, but he still had yet to arrive.

With only a thirty-minute lunch break, I hurriedly wolfed my lunch. Several times I remarked to my friend: "I wonder where Mickey is. Something must have happened." As I excused myself to find a phone, I felt my hands trembling.

Mickey answered the phone at his parents' home. Only then did I breathe a huge sigh of relief. I could tell from his voice he had been asleep.

"Baby, I missed you at lunch. What happened?" I asked.

"What time is it now?"

"Five minutes to one."

"Oh gee, I'm so sorry. I guess I just overslept. Forgive me, please."

"I'm just glad you're all right. I was afraid something might have happened to you."

Mickey's work schedule consisted of twenty-four hours on and forty-eight hours off duty. He had worked the previous night and was clearly worn out. "Well, I'm up now," he said. "I'll be at your house when you get home from work."

When I arrived home, the house was bustling with holiday activities. As usual, Mama and Daddy were sitting at the kitchen table drinking beer with the neighbors, discussing their plans.

Mickey and I sat on the flowered sofa in the living room where we diligently worked to complete seventy-eight thank-you notes.

Later on, David asked, "What are we having for supper?"

We all agreed that take-out burgers sounded good.

Mickey and I headed to Chandlers, our favorite restaurant, and one of the few open on the Fourth of July. We put in Mama's order for two dozen hamburgers at two for a dollar and then headed home. As we rode down Jackson Street, Mickey listened as I vented, "I do wish Mama and Daddy would stop drinking. I don't like seeing them when they drink."

"Maybe someday they will stop," he said. "Let's just keep praying about it. There's one thing for sure, though. At least you won't be living around all that booze much longer. Remember, just nineteen days left until the wedding." The mere thought of remaining at home with my parents' weekend binges brought a familiar knot of dread to my stomach.

Everyone was ravenous by the time we arrived with the food. It wasn't long before I loaded my burger with my favorite fixings and then watched as David ate two hamburgers. Mickey, however, took the prize for putting away four hamburgers.

"Did you get any lunch today?" Daddy asked Mickey.

"No, actually, I didn't," he answered. "I was supposed to eat lunch with Debbie at the hospital cafeteria, but I overslept."

"I know what you mean." Daddy nodded.

The mobile home company where Daddy worked had given him a gorgeous chandelier with five scalloped white globes. After supper, we went to the new house with Daddy to hang the chandelier. Afterward, we stood to admire the beautiful light that completed the interior décor of our little house.

Around 8:30 p.m., Daddy and Mickey, ready to head back to town, gathered their tools. Mickey closed and locked the front door. "Thank God we've finally finished our house," he said. "Now all we have to do is wait for our big day."

Approximately five miles down the road, Mickey suddenly patted his pants pockets, realizing he had locked his keys in the house.

"Oh well, don't worry. I'll let you borrow mine," I offered.

Mickey took out his wallet and handed it to me. "Look inside my wallet, and tell me what you find." At first I thought he meant he had a spare key in his wallet.

"I see your driver's license, your social security card, and six dollars in cash."

"And several pictures of my lovely bride-to-be," he added, smiling.

"Yep, I see them."

"They go everywhere I do."

When we arrived home, I realized I was exhausted. "It sure has been a long day," I told Mickey.

As he sat in Daddy's green rocker recliner, rocking back and forth with me in his lap, I could hardly keep my eyes open. He and David were discussing a movie they wanted to watch. By ten o'clock, I knew I couldn't stay awake another minute.

"Y'all enjoy the movie, guys. I'm off to bed."

I had never gone to bed before Mickey left, but since he and David were watching a movie, I didn't feel the least bit uncomfortable.

I leaned over to give Mickey a goodnight kiss. "I love you, baby. I'll see you tomorrow."

"I love you, too," he said as he squeezed my hand.

"Guess what?" I asked Mickey. Then I softly whispered in his ear, "This is the last holiday before the wedding."

"You're right. The next holiday is Labor Day, and by then we'll be husband and wife."

"I can hardly wait."

"Me either."

Seconds later, I made my way to my bedroom, and within minutes, I was fast asleep.

Later, David reported that Mickey abruptly got up at 10:30 p.m. sharp and told him he was going home. "Don't you want to finish watching the movie?" David asked.

"I don't think so. I really need to get home."

"I thought all your family was at Holiday Beach for the Fourth of July weekend."

"They are, but I'm going to head on to Boston. You can tell me tomorrow how the movie ends."

As Mickey left, David locked the front door and finished watching the movie.

At eleven o'clock, he turned out the lights and joined our parents as they also headed for bed. Shortly the house was quiet, except for Mama's television, which she played all night "to block any outside noises."

Then the telephone rang. At 12:10 a.m. that Sunday morning, Daddy answered the phone, and then woke the entire family. "Mickey is dead. He was killed instantly!"

At age thirteen, David was as mystified as any of us to learn of the accident, especially since he was the last to see Mickey alive.

Daddy hurriedly dressed and drove across town to Danny and Rehberg's home to notify them of the accident.

Just twenty-six minutes after leaving my parents' home, Mickey was killed when his baby blue Volkswagen had been hit head-on. The driver, a twenty-two-year-old male, had been driving under the influence of alcohol. According to the news reports, he was traveling west on U.S. Highway 84 and crossed the center line, apparently forcing several cars off the road before finally hitting Mickey, who was pronounced dead on arrival at 10:56 p.m., July 4, 1976.

The startling news shattered every detailed plan Mickey and I had made over the past seventeen months. In a single moment, his life was snatched away. Mickey was gone—just like that. My life had been turned upside down.

When Mama awakened me with the terrible news, I couldn't believe it. Because I had gone to bed only minutes earlier, I was certain Mickey was still in the living room, watching a movie with David.

*It has to be some kind of a mistake.* I genuinely believed the emergency room staff had confused Mickey with his married older brother, Dave. (Since both Mickey and

I had brothers named David, I refer to my brother as David and Mickey's brother as Dave.) They resembled one another, except for their hair color. Dave had brown hair while Mickey's was blond.

As it turned out, Dave was the only member of his family in town at the time. He was on duty at the fire department. Because I was aware of that fact, I was positive it was Dave who was in the accident.

Unfortunately, I later learned that Dave was dispatched to the scene of the accident, completely unaware that his brother was involved.

As Daddy drove to the emergency room, I prayed the whole way. *God, please don't let it be Mickey. I need him. Our wedding is only nineteen days away.*

"Mama, it just can't be Mickey," I cried out. "He just left our house."

"I know, honey," she said.

"Daddy, it's probably Dave that was in the wreck, don't you think?"

"I don't know, Deb," he answered. "We're almost at the hospital. We'll know soon."

My family and I rushed through the electronic doors to the emergency room desk, where our worst nightmare was confirmed.

"The lady at the information desk said it's Mickey," Daddy whispered, his voice cracking. "His body has been moved to the funeral home."

"I have to go see," I insisted. As Daddy drove out of the parking lot, he made a left turn. Again, the same thought crossed my mind—*Mickey might not be dead!*

"Mama, I love Mickey. I can't live without him." *Oh,*

*God, please don't let Mickey be dead!* The rest of my prayer was lost in my tears.

A tall gentleman at the funeral home confirmed, "Michael Edward McLendon, age twenty-three, was pronounced dead at the scene of the accident nearly two hours ago." At that moment I knew for sure that Mickey was gone.

I wept. "Daddy, I don't want to live without Mickey. Why didn't God take me with him?" I asked, expecting him to have all the answers. "We just rode back together from our house four hours ago. Why didn't the accident happen then?"

By this time, none of the family could speak; we were all in tears.

"We were so happy," I murmured softly to the man at the funeral home. My heart felt like it was breaking in two.

The irony was that Mickey, trained to give aid and comfort to accident victims, was himself a victim of a tragic car accident.

The days immediately following his death were filled with loving memories of our time together. Over and over, my mind replayed the final days and hours leading up to his death.

Just last night, we had enjoyed a wonderful dinner together at the Roman Gate Restaurant, never once thinking it was our last date—and certainly not the last night of his life!

After our meal, Mickey had suggested we drive through downtown Boston. The sleepy little town with a population of approximately 1500 was somewhat unfamiliar to me. I had lived in Thomasville all my life.

"I want to take you to the post office and show you

where our post office box is located," Mickey had said. "Here, try the combination and see if you can open it. Remember, the post office is adjacent to the bank.

"The Citizens & Southern Bank is located off Main Street, and Mr. Aspinwall's hardware store is right over there." He had pointed out the landmarks of the town that would soon be my new home.

"Mr. and Mrs. Tanner live right there. They're really nice people—in case you ever need help.

"Debbie, if something should happen to me, I want you to go back to school to get your RN degree and pay off your Grand Prix," he instructed me.

"Remember that I have two insurance policies. Three weeks ago, I named you as beneficiary of a one thousand-dollar life insurance policy. I have a second policy for twenty thousand dollars with an accidental rider that will be paid to you, my wife. You'll be well taken care of if something should happen to me," he insisted.

I couldn't understand why Mickey was saying these things. All I could think was: *Our wedding is just days away. We have plenty of time to deal with these issues after the wedding*. Then I remembered thinking: *Does Mickey know something I don't?*

After my guided tour of downtown Boston, we had made one final detour to Old Boston Road. With the car headlights shining brightly on the front of our house, we sat in the vehicle, basking in satisfaction of our accomplishments.

A little more than a day later, the remains of his unrecognizable Volkswagen Bug were deposited in an automotive graveyard, its new permanent home.

A death certificate filed at the county hall of records

verified Mickey had died from severe brain damage after suffering a fractured skull and multiple shattered facial bones.

Whispered memories of a drunk driver ... a dead emergency medical technician ... a devastated nurse and a broken-hearted bride-to-be flitted through town for weeks.

Because a cold dark hole was left where my heart had been, I seriously didn't think I could survive the terrible pain of this tragedy. *Why couldn't I have at least had the chance for a proper good-bye?*

On Tuesday morning, July 6, Summerhill Baptist Church was filled with relatives, friends, and flowers—not for our wedding—but for his funeral. Mama, Daddy, and I, along with my brothers, sat on the second pew directly behind Mickey's family.

Reverend Pullen told the congregation that he was thrilled to have been asked to perform our wedding ceremony. "But to have to preach Mickey's funeral instead is one of the hardest things I've ever been asked to do. Mickey and Debbie gave themselves to the things that mattered. They bought and furnished a home—not a mansion, but a modest, comfortable home. They enjoyed making plans for their life together. Mickey enjoyed his work and he enjoyed life."

He was dressed in his favorite blue suit—the one he was to wear when we left the church on our wedding trip. Mickey lay in a blue casket with his favorite picture that would be buried with him at Sunset Gardens.

"Life is good, but it's always temporary, and the best is yet to be," Reverend Pullen said. "We can't blame God for our tragedies. This tragedy wouldn't have happened if God had not allowed it to happen, planning to use it in some way to bless someone."

Twelve gorgeous red roses stood in a spray beside Mickey's casket, along with my handwritten card that read: *To My Darling Mickey. I will love you always. Love, Debbie.*

Within a week after the accident, each person who was to provide a service for our wedding refunded our money: the florist, photographer, even the hotel manager and the Disney World box office agent, who both graciously cancelled our reservations. Each fully understood the sad circumstances. Their kindness touched my heart in a mighty special way.

The checks with our new married name were shredded by the bank officials, except the one I kept to place in my scrapbook.

I notified the post office clerk in Boston. "Cancel Post Office Box two-five-one," I told the lady on the phone. "Without Mickey, I don't need a Boston address or a post office box."

In my purse, I found a ticket stub Mickey had given me from Revco Drug Store. Ten days earlier, he had dropped off the film from our first two bridal showers. A week after his funeral I picked up the photos with the sad realization that he would never see them.

My most anticipated lingerie shower, scheduled to take place four days after his death, and the July 16 Bridesmaids' Luncheon were also cancelled.

The telephone service was cancelled. It would never ring—at least not for Mickey and me.

The morning of July 23, on what would have been our wedding day, I received a lovely bouquet of flowers from Mr. Jimmy. Along with the flowers was a small sixty-one-page hardback book, written by Charles L. Allen. It was titled *When You Lose a Loved One*.

Inside the cover of the book Mr. Jimmy had written:

> *Debbie, I just wanted you to know that I'm thinking of you today. Read page sixteen. I sincerely hope it will help you through the years.*
>
> *In Christian Love,*
> *Jimmy*

That same afternoon I read every word in that tiny book. It stirred my soul and provided me with words of encouragement along with a grand and glorious vision of Mickey's new home in heaven.

Many nights I cried and questioned God. Why had He allowed this to happen? Mickey and I loved each other dearly; it all seemed so right, so perfect.

Remembering the minister's words at Mickey's funeral, "The best is yet to be," I often wondered how anything could be better than Mickey and me becoming husband and wife.

A painful thought hit me—I had not seen the end of living with my parents' weekend alcohol binges. It was then that I became angry with God!

*What will I do now?*

Only God could provide the answers. My personal relationship with Him would help me to survive my terrible loss and, in time, help me to find purpose.

On the night of the Fourth of July, 1976, the party life ended for one of my parents. Mama didn't make a public announcement declaring she had quit drinking, but we children noticed immediately when one weekend after another passed without any booze or partying.

After a month we realized the change was permanent. The prayer Mickey and I had prayed had now been answered. I recalled his words, "Debbie, let's pray that your parents will quit drinking soon. I honestly don't know what it'll take for both of them to see what it's doing to them, to their marriage, and to you and your brothers."

Both my parents struggled with Mickey's death. In fact, Daddy often commented what a good boy Mickey was. "He had his whole life ahead of him," Daddy said. "I wonder why it was cut short." However, the impact wasn't as life-changing for Daddy as it was for Mama. He continued to drink and progressed from weekend binges to chronic alcoholism.

I recalled the minister's words at Mickey's funeral: "The tragedy would not have happened if God had not allowed it to happen, to use it in some way to bless someone."

That someone was *my mother*, who never drank another drop. The loss of an innocent life changed the atmosphere in our home, finally making it possible for me to live more comfortably at home after Mickey's death.

---

"If we grasp the joy of reunion, we
can better handle separation."
*Anonymous*

# Chapter 9

## Letting Go of the House

"The bird of paradise alights only upon
the hand that does not grasp."
*John Berry*

The house, although we had never lived in it, was ours, and it was *ready* to be our home. But without Mickey, I didn't need the house. Without him, it was just like any other ordinary framed house wrapped in white vinyl siding with black shutters. The fact was, there was no way I could afford the mortgage on my small nurse's salary. Besides, I'd never feel safe eight miles from town, all alone in the country.

Since the house was deeded in Mickey's name and we had not yet married, his parents assumed full responsibility for it. As far as I was concerned, they could sell it.

But what would happen to the furnishings and the wedding gifts? For me, the fond memories of our stuff gave me a sense of peace. The things Mickey and I had together represented our love for one another. In my mind, I could see our desolate house, just outside of

Boston, full of unused furniture and wedding gifts. It was a painful vision.

Mama, Aunt Wilma, and our neighbor, Martha, a dear family friend, thought it was best if I went ahead and took care of the items left in the house while I could muster the courage.

I respected Aunt Wilma's advice since she had lost her only son in a car wreck when he was eighteen years old. "The sooner you take care of things, the better off you'll be," she suggested. "The task will allow you time inside the house to deal with your emotions."

Since I had to return to work in twelve days, I decided to take care of business as soon as possible.

Mama thought Thursday, two days after the funeral, was an ideal day to begin the process. She knew that was the day originally planned for my lingerie shower. Sorting through the wedding gifts would likely keep my mind off another disappointment.

To some degree, I dreaded the thoughts of packing the house. I couldn't fathom dismantling all that Mickey and I had worked so hard to accomplish; in some ways, it felt like another death. On the other hand, I longed to see our home fully furnished with everything in its proper place—one last time.

I phoned Mickey's mother to discuss the plan. She agreed to meet us at the house to face the anguish together. We both knew it had to be done. I knew Mickey would want life to go on both for his family and for me.

Mama's oldest brother agreed to haul the furniture in his cattle truck. That is, all except Mickey's bedroom suite, the family heirloom. I intended to pack my wedding gifts, which I knew would mean sobbing my way through the memories of each and every item I touched.

I remembered Mickey's words about the one thousand-dollar life insurance policy. He had mentioned another policy, but I didn't recall the specific details. With proceeds from the first policy, I hoped I'd have enough money to buy a metal building to place in my parents' backyard. The idea of having my furnishings and wedding gifts nearby comforted me.

Mickey's mother, his older sister, and her husband arrived at the same time we did. I used my key to unlock the door. Mickey's key was still locked in the house from Sunday evening.

I opened the door and slowly entered the house. Seeing all the gifts and furnishings immediately brought pain so deep that my dark sunglasses could not hide my swollen, teary eyes. There it was: A furnished home decorated to perfection—never to be occupied—at least not by Mickey and me. It was more than I could bear.

Mickey's family hadn't seen the house since we had added the final touches. I was eager to show them all we had accomplished the past three months.

His mother and sister went straight to the kitchen. Moments later, his mother stormed into the front bedroom where I sat on the bed packing wedding gifts. Her cold and offensive words followed: "Just take everything, Debbie. I know you didn't love Mickey. If you did, you couldn't be here today cleaning out this house before his body gets cold!"

I was speechless, unable to believe what I was hearing. Within thirty minutes, the county sheriff arrived and placed a padlock on the front door. He told everyone to leave the premises until a settlement could be reached. Mama, Aunt Wilma, Martha, and I witnessed the sheer devastation on each others' faces. To this day, I have no recollection of who phoned the police or the events leading up to such drastic action.

My parents were very close to Mickey, and neither of them knew how to handle the bizarre situation. Mama suggested that perhaps Uncle Dick could intervene.

But Mickey's mother had already contacted a local attorney to handle the case. Over time, Uncle Dick also contacted his attorney friend to assist in the matter, but my memories of that day are a complete blur. At the age of nineteen, I was clueless as to how to resolve the unfortunate issues I now faced.

In hopes of settling the case without a court proceeding, the attorneys called Mr. Aspinwall to testify. The attorneys wanted to know his perception of my financial participation in the investment. Mr. Aspinwall told them he witnessed Mickey and me laboring together to make a home. "Both work-wise and money-wise," he said. "They had high hopes of making the house their future home," he confirmed.

Fortunately, Mr. Aspinwall informed the attorneys he had received a fifteen hundred-dollar check with my signature, four months before Mickey's death, to pay for an additional tract of land we bought adjacent to the house.

A little over two months after the incident, I was awarded my cherished items: the wedding gifts, the furniture, and a fifteen hundred-dollar refund check to cover the land purchase that was now part of the real property.

On that same day, the attorneys made their final decision: the house, the additional land, and the bedroom set was given to Mickey's family, along with one wedding gift that its owner had asked to be returned.

The gift itself wasn't so important. However, I felt a terrible weight of sadness when I learned it was a member of Mickey's family who demanded their gift be returned. A few months later, Mickey's sister and her husband made the house their home.

With the proceeds of the one thousand-dollar insurance policy, I paid the five hundred-dollar attorney fee and spent $498 to purchase the building to store my possessions.

Because the second policy Mickey mentioned did not have a named beneficiary, it was automatically paid to the next of kin.

The day after Mickey's death, I recall his mother suggesting the family and I take the Disney World trip the week of July 23. But after the incident, no one ever mentioned it again.

Since my loss was bad enough already, without additional heartache, I desperately tried to understand the abrupt behavior changes I observed. As a relatively new nurse, I recalled reading about the various ways individuals handle grief. I wanted to believe Mickey's family's actions were speaking out of pain and not merely a dislike for me. I hoped and prayed the issues could be resolved. Only then could peace be restored and true healing really begin.

Although I truly felt no bitterness in my heart, I knew Mickey wouldn't be happy with our broken relationship. I prayed that someday things would be right again, to benefit us all.

---

"When one is out of touch with
oneself, one cannot touch others."
*Anne Morrow Lindbergh*

# Chapter 10

## Finding Purpose After Loss

"Build up, build up, prepare the road! Remove the obstacles out of the way of my people."
*Isaiah 57:14*

The sun always shines after the rain.

After the news of Mickey's death circulated through the small town of Boston, as well as neighboring towns, I received a bundle of cards and letters—all with messages of hope and encouragement.

Many of the remembrances came from patients I nursed on Two West. They diligently tried to identify themselves by sharing information about their illnesses or by identifying their room numbers. Realizing that people, especially my former patients, cared and prayed for me lifted my spirits immensely.

Five days after Mickey's death I received two condolences that genuinely touched my heart:

*You probably don't remember me, but I was a patient in a ward with an old colored woman, a*

*Hurst girl, and another old woman. You were my nurse for several days, and I said several times you were so nice and such a good nurse. I remember your name, and you told me you were going to be married in July. I saw this piece in the Thomasville paper; I just knew it was your boyfriend. I also saw your picture and the article in yesterday's paper. Debbie, I love you and feel so sorry for you. May God bless and take care of you. He is the One you have to look to in times of troubles. If ever I am back at the hospital, I will try to see you. I will pray for you. Time alone can heal your many heartaches. God bless you.*

*I know with the many patients you've had you probably don't remember me. I had a broken wrist on February twenty-fifth. You were so kind and attentive to me, and my husband and I were so grateful. We are sad to learn of the tragedy and your loss. We will be praying for you.*

Another card came from the patient who gave us our very first wedding card and our first wedding gift. I had never expected words of sympathy to replace words of congratulations.

As I read the message, I recalled Mickey's final words to me: "Become a Registered Nurse." Realizing a former patient and her daughter were willing to help me in my endeavor was a vivid reminder of their care and concern:

*Just hope these words of sympathy are able to convey the thought that others understand and share your loss today. We love you very much and were so sorry to hear what happened. Remember that my daughter, Peggy, will be living, working, and going to school in Atlanta. If and when you decide to go back to nursing school, we would be glad to give you all the information we have and help you as much as we can. If you ever need us for anything, please call on us. I think you are a very fine young lady.*

Returning to work on the orthopedic unit, I immediately reflected on my conversation with Mickey regarding my future in his absence. "Pay off your car. Go back to school." His words echoed in my mind for days, even months. The instructions seemed so simple. However, I faced a huge quandary.

How could I honor Mickey's wishes when I didn't have the money? The wedding refunds and the $1,500 land refund were a far cry from the amount I needed to finance my education. With a small nurse's salary and monthly car payments, I wasn't sure how to accomplish my goal. But one thing I did know for certain: I was determined to become a professional nurse.

The following months I explored every avenue possible to acquire the money. My first big decision was the selection of the right school. Although I had always dreamed of attending the Medical College of Georgia, I knew that was an unlikely consideration, because I expected to come home at least two weekends each month to work at the hospital.

My friend Sheree was attending Georgia Southwestern College to become a nurse. That was a more viable option since Americus was located only two hours away.

I contacted the admissions department and learned

that the approximate annual cost of a nursing education totaled three thousand dollars. In just two years I could earn an associate degree, and by the summer of 1979, I'd be eligible to sit for the State Board exam to become licensed as an RN. I became excited.

Since school would start in September, only two months after Mickey's death, it was impossible to complete all the necessary paperwork, obtain the funds, and equip myself in that short time period. Besides, I was still dealing with the house issues—those that *had* to be settled before I could focus on studying and learning.

I was completely satisfied with the plan to start school the following September. By living with my parents for another year, I was able to make extra car payments and raise the tuition.

Since I was employed by the hospital for almost a year prior to Mickey's death, I started my quest for financial aid by researching the hospital benefit package. An annual one thousand-dollar scholarship was available through the Beard Scholarship Fund. Returning to work at the hospital for two consecutive years following graduation would void the repayment of the scholarship.

The Georgia Higher Education Nursing Scholarship Fund would provide an annual tuition of two thousand dollars. If I continued to work in nursing for two years in Georgia, they would forgive repayment of that debt as well.

Therefore, I quickly calculated: If I returned to work at the hospital after graduation, I'd be working in the State of Georgia, and ultimately my education would be paid in full. I loved the idea from the moment of its inception.

Then I received the best news yet. Mama's employer at the record store was also a guidance counselor at Thomas

Tech. He informed me of a possible grant available through the Georgia Department of Labor. The financial assistance program was available for students with a high GPA who wished to further their education.

"You mean I'll be paid to go to nursing school?" I asked the woman at the labor office.

"Yes, Debbie, you are eligible for the CETA grant. You will receive a check for eighty dollars every week as long as you're enrolled in school."

The CETA paycheck settled my car payment dilemma, and it also provided spending money. Interestingly enough, the year I graduated was the final year that grant was made available in the State of Georgia.

That long year working at the hospital while waiting to go to college was extremely difficult, as waves of sadness hit me again and again. It seemed that everywhere I turned at the hospital I saw Mickey. In my deep grief, I went to work and then I went home. It was as simple as that.

Mickey's sister and I had graduated from the same practical nursing class at Tech. She also worked at the hospital. I remember the day we met while delivering the daily census report to the nursing office. Just as we passed the entrance, she used an obscenity to address me.

The ladies working in the business office, adjacent to the nursing office, overheard her ugly comment. Appalled, I chose not to respond. The following day, at different times, we were each called to the nursing office. The nursing director reminded me that any outside feelings should not be brought to work. However, she assured me that she was aware of the sad circumstances that had taken place since Mickey's death.

I had many friends at the hospital, yet I felt abandoned.

The truth of the matter was, I felt like a widow. As far as I was concerned, I was a widow! Mickey was as much a husband as if we had been married. The only difference was, we had saved ourselves for marriage. To both of us, that was an important part of our identity as a couple.

I recall my visits with Martha, who was like a second mom. She was working as secretary on the same unit where I worked as a nurse. One day while we were talking, she asked me, "Debbie, do you think you'll ever get married?"

"No, Martha. I seriously doubt there will ever be anyone else in my life." My answer to that question was always the same, because that was truly how I felt.

Although I had to attend church *alone*, I became a faithful member of Temple Baptist Church. At that time the small congregation was meeting in the chapel of a local funeral home. I remember the pastor teasing me about parking my car in the nearby convenience store parking lot and walking to church. The distance wasn't that great; it was simply his way of letting me know he appreciated my faithfulness. To this day, I have utmost respect for the godly man my family and I refer to as Preacher Coram.

His sermons and encouragement gave me the strength to live life without Mickey. I started reading and studying my Bible daily. Romans 8:28 brought significant comfort as I trusted God had a purpose in this situation.

In October 1976, three months after the tragedy, Billy and his wife, Kathy, were expecting their first baby. Shortly after Kimberly was born they invited me to spend a few days with them in South Carolina. They realized the turmoil I was experiencing.

For the first time in my life, I rode on a Greyhound

bus, sitting directly behind the male bus driver all the way to Summerville. Although I didn't learn his name, I'll never forget the gentleman's kindness and concern. By this time, I was desperate for someone to talk to, and his listening ear during the six-hour ride allowed me a chance to share my feelings. That was the beginning of my healing process.

The following September I was ready to start school. I soon realized my LPN training had set the groundwork for my ongoing nursing career.

*My first year in college. I trimmed my long hair a little but was still wearing "thick" glasses.*

The two years of college provided many memorable moments and healing opportunities. I developed two special friendships: Robin from Hawkinsville and Jenny, who called Macon home. Together the three of us joined the Zeta Tau Alpha sorority.

Robin and I shared a dorm suite on the sorority floor at the college. Later she decided to get an outside apartment, leaving me with a private room, which I greatly enjoyed. Jenny lived a few doors from me on the Zeta floor.

Being part of a sorority required paying monthly dues. It was a comfort knowing I had a weekly paycheck sufficient to pay my obligation. During my time there, I fulfilled all the required duties of the sorority and was blessed to be the recipient of the "Most Outstanding Pledge" award. At the completion of my pledge experience, I also received the "Highest Scholastic Award" among pledges. These awards increased the confidence I had begun to feel as a result of Mickey's love.

In my sophomore year I was elected to the position of secretary for the Association for Women Students. Although I still struggled with shyness, I was so focused on fulfilling my promise to Mickey that I seldom thought of my weakness.

My hectic school schedule left little time to dwell on painful memories. Not only was I preparing well for my future as a nurse, but I found inexplicable peace and purpose as I honored Mickey's last request.

Working two part-time jobs became excellent therapy for me—especially since I had no love life. I traveled two hundred miles round trip every other weekend to work at the hospital at home. On alternate weekends, I was employed by Magnolia Manor in Americus, my first experience working in a nursing home. It didn't take long for me to realize that I loved working in geriatrics.

During the final week of my first year of college, Dr. Blackman, my friend and optometrist back home, called to tell me the good news: contact lenses were finally being manufactured in a minus-ten prescription! With a new goal in mind, I quickly saved enough to afford the purchase of the new contacts. With graduation only a year away, I was thrilled to realize I'd be wearing contacts at the commencement. Even more so, I'd also begin my professional nursing career—without glasses!

Since I was changing my look, I decided it was also the perfect time to shorten my long brown hair. My peers hardly recognized me when I returned to school for the final year.

*Nurse Pinning Ceremony: My looks changed and my classmates hardly recognized me.*

That same year, I received notification that the Beard Scholarship was increasing from one thousand dollars to two thousand dollars. "I know you will soon graduate," said the kind gentleman, "but you are eligible to receive the additional two thousand dollars in a lump sum. Perhaps it will help you as you begin your career. The only requirement is that you fulfill your two-year work commitment to the hospital."

With the assistance of those additional funds, I paid off my car debt and established my first real savings account during the last quarter of school. Continuing the trait I had learned as a child, I spent wisely and responsibly.

On June 21, 1979, I proudly walked the aisle to receive my Associate in Arts Degree. Wearing a black cap and gown with a peach-colored tassel gave me an immense feeling of accomplishment and self-worth. I was now a Graduate Nurse and eligible to sit for the state board exam. Soon I could start my practice as a Registered Nurse.

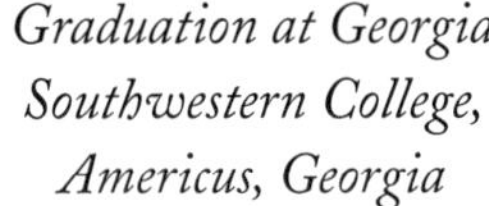

*Graduation at Georgia Southwestern College, Americus, Georgia*

The two years at Georgia Southwestern provided immeasurable benefits at a time when I needed them most. The day immediately following graduation was bittersweet. I packed all my personal belongings and moved from my sorority suite.

As hard as it was, I knew moving back home was the right decision. Daddy's continued drinking problem had taken its toll. Two months earlier my parents' divorce became final. While Mama needed my financial help, my teenage brother needed my emotional support.

Before leaving the campus, I made one final trip up the three flights of stairs, skipping a step as I climbed to the top. Re-entering my dorm suite for the last time, I sat quietly on the stripped twin bed. Although my belongings were loaded in the car and the room was vacant, it was anything but empty. A sense of peace filled the space around me. I felt a sublime sense of contentment. Tears of joy filled my eyes as I recalled all that had occurred since Mickey's death. Quietly thanking God, I realized He had been there all the time. It was His plan for me to become a registered nurse from the very beginning. Now it was time for me to go back home.

---

"We must be willing to let go of the life we've planned, so as to have the life that is waiting for us."
*Joseph Campbell*

---

Although Mickey had gone to be with the Lord, I still held tightly to the memories of our time together. We had something very special between us that no one could ever take away.

## In Memoriam–July 4, 1977

In loving memory of my fiancé, Michael Edward McLendon, who departed this life one year ago, July 4, 1976.

*This year has been lonely*
*Since you went away,*
*But I'll always give thanks to God*
*For giving you to me to love*
*Till death did us part.*
*And then I ask for added strength*
*To live with my broken heart;*
*Each day I remind myself*
*How blessed I really was.*
*For many live a lifetime*
*Without knowing such a love.*
*It broke my heart to lose you,*
*But you did not go alone,*
*For part of me went with you…*
*The day God called you home.*
*Peaceful be thy sleep, dear.*
*It is sweet to breathe your name,*
*In life I loved you dearly—*
*In death I do the same.*
Sadly missed by your fiancée, Debbie, and family.

---

"Those we love are with the Lord, and the Lord has promised to be with us; if they are with Him and He is with us, they cannot be far away."
*Anonymous*

# Chapter 11
## The Man I Call Bo

"Success in marriage is more than finding the right person. It's becoming the right person."
*Anonymous*

Finally, becoming a registered nurse opened up a whole new world to me. Immediately after graduation, I accepted a full-time leadership position on the evening shift at Archbold Memorial Hospital. As charge nurse of the IV team, I enjoyed circulating through the hospital to administer IV meds while visiting with my patients. Returning to work at the hospital eliminated the need to repay my scholarships. I was happy as a lark with that arrangement, finally making good money and not owing a dime to anyone.

On the other hand, graduating from college without a steady boyfriend or the possibility of a life's mate reminded me of a previous discussion I had years before with my neighbor and coworker, Martha. Maybe our thoughts were right on target: The likelihood of finding a new soul mate was slim to none. The thought of being alone for the rest of my life seemed very disheartening.

During my college days, I dated a couple of guys without much zeal. The Zeta annual formal dance, known as Silver Crown, prompted me to invite a friend to share the special night. I remember Charlie, the first young man I bumped into one day at lunch in the college cafeteria. "He's so nice, so kind," I shared with Jenny.

"Why don't you ask him to go to Silver Crown?" she suggested. I couldn't imagine doing that. Just the thought of asking out a guy frightened me beyond words. *Mickey was my lifelong love. Dating other guys just doesn't feel right.*

Nonetheless, for two consecutive days Jenny pushed me. "Charlie is waiting for you to ask him to Silver Crown. He thinks you're pretty, and besides, you are shorter than him. He likes that. You two would make a cute couple."

"What if he says no?" I asked, feeling skeptical.

"Well then, you can find someone else," she replied. "But I don't think you have anything to worry about. Just trust me." It all sounded so easy.

It was my first year as a Zeta sister. As recipient of the Outstanding Pledge award, my participation was not optional at the formal dance. I knew I couldn't fail to show up.

I finally mustered the nerve to ask Charlie, and he quickly accepted my invitation. I later discovered Jenny had it all planned just that way. That was okay though. I needed a little push—or maybe a big shove.

Deep in my heart I trusted that there was a special someone out there, somewhere, just for me. I believed both Mickey and God wanted that for me—one who would treat me with the dignity and respect Mickey had shown me during our time together.

Occasionally, I found myself hoping and praying I'd find a husband, but I knew I was on the road to emotional recovery when I could finally trust my desire to God.

Since I worked evenings, I generally visited with Mama each morning at the record shop. I always stopped by Rose City Bakery and bought six glazed donuts for our mid-morning snack.

At least three or four times every week the record shop received a large delivery of records, albums, and tapes. A handsome dark-haired UPS man with striking blue eyes delivered the packages. I noticed that he seemed to hurriedly deliver the boxes up and down Jackson Street before he made his way to the record store.

Out of the blue, the UPS guy named Bo began to stay for longer periods of time each morning. He ate donuts right along with us, and some mornings before I got to the shop he was already there with a dozen donuts. *Waiting on me?* I wondered. He called this respite his lunch break.

Mama visited with Bo more than I did, especially since the two of them had something in common. She and Daddy had been divorced a little over a year, while Bo had recently been through a terrible divorce. The early lunch stop allowed him valuable time to share his feelings with us.

Bo proudly called himself a Cajun; his family was still in the Bayou State where he had been raised. His upbeat personality and easy laugh kept us smiling so that we loved to see him come.

*My own "personal" UPS man with his striking blue eyes.*

After working for six months as an RN, I debated about buying a new 1980 blue Grand Prix. Uncle Dick sensed my novice insecurity. "If you want a new vehicle, then get it," he said. "You're making enough to pay the note."

"But there isn't anything wrong with the '76 Grand Prix I have now. I just like the new body style, that's all."

Reluctantly, I made the decision to purchase the newer model with payments of $180 a month. It stirred the same kind of anxious feelings I'd experienced after Mickey's death when I wondered how I'd pay for my car *and* attend nursing school.

*I can afford it now*, I kept telling myself. Spending money was no easy task for me, as I'd learned frugality from an early age.

"When are you going to take me for a ride in your new car?" Bo asked while leaning on the counter in the record shop, enjoying his third cup of coffee.

From our previous morning conversations, I learned he was the new owner of a gray and black Harley Sportster motorcycle.

"When are you going to take me for a ride on your motorcycle?" I quickly fired back.

Without a moment of hesitation, he replied, "I'll pick you up Saturday morning, and we'll ride the country roads."

As it turned out, Saturday was the absolute coldest day of the winter in south Georgia. Nonetheless, I wasn't about to refuse the promised ride. And although I had never ridden on a motorcycle, I wasn't the least bit afraid.

For some strange reason, this guy interested me. I sensed there was something authentic about him.

"Do you like him?" asked Mama.

"Oh, he's okay. But you know he's been married before, and I will not seriously date any man who's been divorced."

"Well, I'm divorced," Mama replied with a knowing frown.

"I know, but . . . "

One day when Mama's boss was in the shop, he began asking questions. "So how's it going with the UPS man?"

"I'm just not too sure about him. He's been married before, and I'm *not* going to get serious about a divorced man."

"That doesn't make him a bad person," Mr. Len remarked. "Now you think about it, Debbie. He seems like a good ol' boy to me. He's just been through a rough spell, that's all."

Neither Mama nor Mr. Len was fooled by my act. The truth of the matter was, I liked the UPS man, and the UPS man liked me.

As the weeks passed, our attachment to one another grew stronger. The two of us had similar likes and dislikes.

The question was whether or not I could accept him as a divorcee, the father of two minor children. Then one spring day it hit me.

Bo had endured a significant loss in his life. Although he had a biblical reason for his divorce, he faced that painful disappointment every day of his life. Not only was the divorce difficult for him, but so was the separation from the daughter and son he dearly loved.

As far as I was concerned, I still carried the title of widow. And though my loss was quite different from that which Bo felt, I realized, *A loss is a loss.*

Then I remembered my parents' difficult issues. Neither of them were bad people. I wondered why I felt so strongly about the issue. If my relationship with Bo was to flourish, I realized I had to get past these preconceived notions. That very day I began to pray for my heart to change.

Bo and I planned to be married on September 6, 1980. Our wedding invitations were printed; everything was in perfect order.

On a Friday afternoon, two months prior to our wedding, Bo received a dreadful phone call from his brother: "Bo, you need to come home. Daddy just shot himself in the head. He's dead!"

Bo was devastated. I was glad I could be there for him. He faced that horrible empty ache that never quite goes away. I knew exactly how it felt never to have had the chance for a proper good-bye.

After making the necessary funeral arrangements earlier that day, Bo's dad had written and mailed letters to family members and friends in advance of taking his own life. Bo received the final letter from his dad three days after the shooting. Sadly, I never met my future father-in-law who had addressed his letter to Bo and Debbie.

Following the funeral service and committal, we made the decision to move our wedding date up to early August. Delaying the wedding wasn't even a remote possibility—not for me. It made no difference that our wedding invitations were dated September 6. I simply crossed through the date and wrote the new date, August 8. The blue wedding napkins with the wrong date didn't matter either. Putting things off was simply not an option.

After Mr. Griffiths' death, Bo's mother had to depend on her older son and his wife, a school teacher, to bring her to the wedding. If our wedding didn't take place before school started in early September, she would not have been able to attend.

Before we married, Bo and I had a true heart-to-heart regarding two very important issues. We both realized the motorcycle had to go since the monthly payments didn't fit our budget.

"Maybe someday when I retire I'll buy another motorcycle," he said. I liked that idea since I enjoyed riding just as much as he did.

The other issue involved church attendance. Bo had accepted Christ at the age of twenty-eight, and I found comfort knowing he was a Christian. But after his divorce, he stopped attending his former church, which I could certainly understand. But he promised, reiterating in our wedding vows: "Our Christian home will be one of much love and understanding." For us, that meant worshiping weekly in God's house.

*Aunt Wilma and Uncle Dick at our wedding*

The most difficult part in planning for our wedding was finding a pastor who was willing to officiate a wedding in which one of the parties had gone through divorce. Finally, after being turned down by several clergy, we were very pleased when my sister-in-law's brother, the Reverend DeWitt Rehberg, willingly agreed to marry us. He listened to all that had happened in Bo's life. He knew of my own tragic loss four years earlier. With heartfelt compassion, DeWitt agreed to officiate at our wedding.

Eight months after our first date, I married my own personal UPS man. We were united in a gorgeous outdoor ceremony in the yard of our Raleigh Avenue home on the eighth month and the eighth day of 1980. Four years, four weeks, and four days after Mickey's death, my little brother gave me away.

*August 8, 1980. Mama and little brother, David, gave me away.*

Unfortunately, Daddy was still struggling with alcohol abuse, now more than ever. Not only could I not depend on him to be sober, but I knew that he and Mama couldn't set foot on the same soil without inviting disaster. Having both parents present for my cherished day, with Daddy there to give me away, was a dream I never realized.

Although Bo was eight years older than me, the age difference never bothered either of us. Because of our losses, we discovered we could relate in ways other couples could not.

For the first time since Mickey's death, I felt safe in the arms of someone special, sent just for me, who loved me as much as Mickey had. I knew Bo would treat me with the dignity and respect that I had come to cherish.

I knew without a doubt that he would support me in any endeavor I chose, just as I was the woman who would support him following a trying divorce and all that went with it.

On Halloween Day in October 1982, Bo and I became the proud parents of a darling baby boy. Shortly after birth, Kyle was diagnosed with a collapsed lung. Physicians were concerned he may not survive. I also experienced health issues and was transferred from the OB wing to a medical unit. Miraculously, Kyle and I were discharged seven days later from the hospital. It quickly became clear that my health wouldn't allow us to have more children.

As I crawled into our king-size waterbed that night, I felt a huge sigh of relief. Both Kyle and I were finally home and healthy.

At age twenty-five, I was geared and ready for the duties of motherhood, thrilled with the special little guy who had become a part of our world. During my pregnancy we had planned well so I could stay at home for the first six months of his life.

Daddy called with a happy announcement the same night I arrived home from the hospital. "Deb, I called to congratulate you on the birth of my new grandson and to tell you—the day your son was born was the day I stopped drinking!"

I was thrilled beyond words to hear Daddy's good news, but only time would tell if he truly meant what he said. My experience as a nurse taught me he might relapse at any time. However, over the next few months, he was sober every time I saw him. He never went back on his word; his addiction to alcohol stopped just like that.

After he lost his driver's license from numerous DUI charges, Daddy bought a bicycle so he could get to and from work at Liberty Homes. On those bitter cold mornings, Bo, on his way to work, often met Daddy coming across London Bridge on his bike. He stopped his truck, put Dad's bike in his pick-up, and took him to work. Since Daddy had kept his promise to remain sober, Bo and I assisted him financially with the purchase of a mobile home. In fact, he was still living there that dreadful day years later when he called crying for help.

Like a son to my parents, Bo was always there to help me as I struggled with my dysfunctional family issues. As a father, he gently nurtured our son as much as I did: changing his diapers, feeding him supper, and rocking him to sleep, all while I worked.

A more attentive and generous husband I could never have found: a beautiful example of Christ's love for His Bride, the Church.

*The man I call Bo* picked up exactly where Mickey left off.

---

"Submit to one another out of reverence for Christ."
*Ephesians 5:21*

# Chapter 12

## Call to Long-Term Care

"You gain strength, courage, and confidence by every experience in which you really stop to look fear in the face. You are able to say to yourself, 'I lived through this horror. I can take the next thing that comes along.'"

*Eleanor Roosevelt*

*Don't Regret Growing Old–It's a Privilege Denied to Many.* That was the adage written on the small and fragile four-by-five-inch plaque hanging in the domestics section of Roses Department Store.

Mama and I were browsing when I caught a glimpse of the plaque—shaped like an ice cream scoop hanging on a rack at the end of the aisle. As I turned the corner with my shopping cart, I drew close enough to read the words.

Immediately, I felt a sentimental connection. It seemed as though the words were speaking to me, although I didn't understand why. I carefully placed the plaque in the shopping cart, unable to leave without it.

When we arrived home, I wrapped it tightly and placed it in the top of my chest of drawers, unwilling for it to get broken. Like all my keepsakes, I hoped to have the chance to display it one day.

After our marriage, I continued working evenings at the hospital, while Bo stayed at his job as a UPS driver. Sometimes we felt like we only waved at each other, coming and going, waiting patiently for my turn to land a daytime job.

My old friend Linda Hancock buttonholed me one day not too long after Kyle was born. "Listen, there's an opening for a director of nurses at Camellia Gardens Nursing Home. I heard the current nursing director resigned, and I immediately thought of you, Debbie. I can see you ministering right there ... and now, you're the first person I see this afternoon. Girlfriend, go check it out!"

After working together at the hospital three years earlier, Linda had taken a position as nursing instructor at the tech school. But we still had a common thread—our love for nursing, our special *calling*. We both graduated from LPN school prior to becoming registered nurses, and we always went above and beyond the call of duty to meet the needs of our patients.

I stood at the Two East nurse's station browsing the medical chart of one of my assigned patients. While Linda and I chatted, her charge to me continued. "I hear you're doing a great job on the IV team, but serving as the nursing director could open a whole new world for you. Besides, it's a day position. It's a grand opportunity just waiting for you."

"Uh, it sounds great, Linda, but you know I love working

at the hospital. I've already invested nine years, and I'm not too sure I'd like working in a nursing home."

"Oh well, just pray about it. Follow your heart. God will show you the way."

"Thanks for the information. I'll check on it."

*I doubt I'll ever check it out,* I thought. Me, the director of nurses? I couldn't even imagine that, not in my wildest dreams.

"Okay, girl, let me know what you find out. I'll be thinking about you. Gotta go. I've got students on Five West. Don't work too hard."

As Linda moseyed down the hallway toward the elevator, my mind constantly replayed her words of advice. *Work in a nursing home? Serve as director of nurses?*

I never doubted that God called me into nursing, but I wasn't sure working in a skilled nursing facility was a choice I would make if given the opportunity.

But as a young wife and the mother of a fourteen-month-old son, I could see how wonderful it would be to work the day shift. I relished the idea of being home with my family. Working evenings and weekends was becoming increasingly more difficult with a child. Not only that, my work schedule prevented us from ever attending evening church services.

Although I didn't seriously consider applying for the job at the time, I did subconsciously begin evaluating my strengths. I had always felt more comfortable around people older than myself. As a child, I had enjoyed sitting at the kitchen table with Mama and her lady friends, listening to their chats. I thought about the front porch visits with Grandma and Grandpa and recalled the great times I had at Furney Farm.

As far as my nursing experiences, I loved visiting with my elderly patients, slowly administering their IV meds to allow time to chat with each one. Both patients and co-workers often mentioned the gift I had for relating to the elderly.

*Could this director position be meant for me? Can I make a difference?* I wondered. I felt frightened just thinking about it.

Linda was unaware that behind my hesitation, I felt a deep fear of leadership. Working independently as an IV nurse never made me face my phobia. A leadership role in a nursing home would definitely force me into the spotlight.

Flipping the pages of Mr. Smith's medical chart, I searched diligently for the physician's order sheet. A quick review told me he was an eighty-six-year-old, admitted with dehydration and a possible urinary tract infection.

"Good afternoon, Mr. Smith. My name is Debbie, and I'll be your IV nurse this afternoon. I'm sorry you aren't feeling well. Do you mind if I pull up a chair? I'll sit here beside your bed while I administer the antibiotic. It'll only take about five or six minutes."

"I reckon that'll be all right, honey."

After a time, he said, "My wife died a few weeks ago, and I miss her so much." I handed him a tissue to wipe the tears streaming down his cheeks. "She was such a wonderful woman. We did everything together. She was also a great cook. Good ol' collard greens and fried chicken. You know, life won't ever be the same."

"I'm so sorry about the loss of your wife, Mr. Smith. I understand how you feel. Losing a loved one is never easy—especially when it's your soul mate."

"I've gotta bunch of cows and pigs, but only a few

chickens. My wife and I loved the farm. I took care of the bigger animals, while she enjoyed caring for the chickens and gathering the eggs. But she never minded rising early to milk the cows with me when I needed help."

Mr. Smith's story sounded so familiar. "Do you mind if I pray with you, Mr. Smith?" I asked.

Gripping my hand firmly, he replied, "Oh, honey, would you please?"

A minute later I squeezed his hand. "I sure enjoyed my time with you, and I hope you have a wonderful evening. Get some rest now," I suggested as I patted him on the back. Just as I turned to leave the room, I could see tears filling his eyes. He quickly brushed them away.

"Will you please come back to see me tomorrow?" he asked, his face tense.

"Yes, sir, Mr. Smith, I sure will. I'll be working the three-to-eleven shift tomorrow. I'll come by to see you during that time." I gently took his hand in mine, kissed it, and said, "I care about you."

"You are so kind, honey. Thank you," he said. With a smile on his face, an incredible calm seemed to fill his room.

Leaving Mr. Smith's room, I collected the chart of my next patient. While browsing the pages of Mrs. Johnson's medical record, I heard Linda's words echoing in my mind. I played devil's advocate.

*I am satisfied working at the hospital. With nine years of service, why should I consider a job change?*

Two doors down the corridor I met Mrs. Johnson, a white-haired seventy-year-old lady with glistening blue eyes and a loving smile.

"I'm Debbie, and I'll be your IV medication nurse this afternoon. How are you today, Mrs. Johnson?"

"Well, darlin,' I fell down the steps at my daughter's house, and wouldn't you know, I broke my right arm."

"I'm so sorry. But I'm here to help, so you'll be up and going before you know it."

"I sure hope so," she replied. "I lost my husband last Christmas, and I'm dreading the holidays. Because this will be my first holiday without Harvey, I'm going to my daughter's house for dinner on Christmas Day. If I'm able, that is," she said as her voice broke.

"I'm so happy you have a supportive family. Being together on the holidays is so important."

"Yes, darlin,' they'll be there for me, but it'll still be hard without Harvey."

"I'm sure you're right. Believe me, I know how you feel, and I'll be praying for you."

"Thank you, darlin.' You're very sweet."

*Go check it out… check it out…* The words continued to ring in my mind over and over like a refrain.

The next morning I awakened early excited. *Today I'm going to check it out,* I reminded myself. Driving to the nursing home, my mind raced back to my two favorite patients, Mr. Smith and Mrs. Johnson. Spending time with them somehow brought unspeakable joy to my heart, a satisfaction I'd never known until now.

As I drove into the front parking lot of the yellow brick building, a cold shudder ran through me. Feelings of uncertainty surfaced like a bad debt. That inner voice was there again: *You know you can't function as a nursing director. You can scarcely say your name in front of a group.*

Although I wrestled with a host of disconcerting feelings, I confronted my insecurity. *Maybe I can work at the nursing home, but if someone has already been hired for the position, then I'll know for sure the job was not for me.*

Public speaking had always been a challenge for me, so the thought of managing a nursing home seemed way out of my comfort zone. Leading resident and staff meetings and handling family conferences loomed like an impossible task.

"Hello, my name is Debbie Griffiths, and I'm here to apply for the Director of Nurses position," I told the woman in the front office.

"Just have a seat. I'll get Mrs. Kiser for you," she said.

Shortly, the attractive administrator held out her hand in greeting. "Hello, my name is Bobbie Kiser. It's so nice to meet you. Come into the office." She put me at ease with her sweet smile and gentle demeanor.

Mrs. Kiser began to explain the requirements for the position. The individual would function not only as DON, but also as her Assistant Administrator.

"I'm looking for a compassionate, caring, and loving RN who enjoys working with older adults—someone with a big heart, willing to listen to the residents.

"Let's take a quick tour of the facility," she suggested. "That'll give you a better idea of the scope of the position."

As we traipsed down the hall, several ladies and gentlemen placed their hands in mine, and immediately I felt like I'd come home.

"You know, not all nurses can work in a skilled nursing facility," said Mrs. Kiser. "But I'm an RN, and I've always loved long-term care. It's a very rewarding experience."

When we returned to Mrs. Kiser's office, she asked, "Mrs. Griffiths, would you consider accepting the position?

I believe you are just the one we're looking for. You seem sincerely concerned about the residents."

Now my heart raced. "Let me think about it, Mrs. Kiser. I need to discuss it with my husband and pray about it. I'll let you know after lunch tomorrow."

While driving home, I felt overwhelmed with feelings of inadequacy. *Can I really find my niche in this facility?*

I had never once imagined myself, as timid as I am, functioning in such an enormous position of leadership.

Bo and I discussed the job offer and its fringe benefits for our family.

"Accept the position," he said.

"Do you really think I can do it, Bo?" I asked, anxious to hear his opinion. "You know how much I hate speaking in front of groups."

"I don't think you need to worry about it," he replied. "Just take the position and do your best."

Two days later, I saw Linda again at the hospital. I could hardly wait to share my news. "Guess what? I got the job at Camellia Gardens!"

"Congratulations, girlfriend! Starting when?" she asked while lifting her hand for a high five.

"In two weeks—January 9."

"You'll do fine. I told you to follow your heart."

Eleven months later, at the annual Christmas party, Mrs. Kiser took charge of the festivities. Because this was my first celebration with the residents and staff, I wasn't sure of the agenda. I was aware that Mrs. Kiser was planning to draw names because I helped her gather door prizes. I knew she scheduled holiday entertainment, and I knew she planned to honor the "Employee of the Year."

A week earlier, I had submitted my vote for a dedicated nursing assistant to receive the award.

At the recognition ceremony, I was utterly speechless when Mrs. Kiser announced, "The Employee of the Year award goes to—Mrs. Griffiths!" Because of my position, I had no idea I was eligible to win.

She smiled. "We don't ordinarily allow a department head to receive this recognition, but I chose to honor the request of the residents and staff who all voted for you."

Through tears of joy, I shared my sentiments of gratitude—publicly. *What did I do to deserve this honor*? I wondered.

From that time on, I realized God had gifted me with a love of senior adults. Long-term care was indeed my calling.

During our time together, Mrs. Kiser and I became close friends. We worked hard to provide excellent care for our residents and received near-perfect ratings on our state inspection reports. Our facility boasted an outstanding reputation. Working with her, I gained a wealth of knowledge while learning how to successfully manage a long-term care facility.

One morning she and I stopped by Burger King for a quick bite. As we talked, I remember saying, "Bobbie, I really wish I could get past my crazy fears."

"You know, Debbie, I believe you'll overcome them," she said. "And I have a feeling you'll do great things. You've already done more than you ever imagined, haven't you?"

The next two years were years of growth for me at the nursing home. The company allowed me the unique opportunity to participate in Leadership Eighties, a program sponsored by the local Chamber of Commerce. I served on the advisory board for the technical school, my alma mater, and was elected president of the Southwest Georgia Association of Nurses in Long-Term Care, a position I held for two years.

Then corporate made a big announcement. The nursing home, which had always been a private-pay facility, would soon be accepting Medicaid patients. The thought of tackling a mountain of additional paperwork, which inevitably falls in the lap of the DON, didn't appeal to me at all.

Bo and I wondered out loud if this could be happening for a reason.

At that time, the hospital was only weeks away from opening a brand new oncology center, and I briefly entertained the idea of becoming a chemo nurse. With several years experience in both IV nursing and geriatrics, I recalled Linda's words of advice: "Follow your heart." Her words of guidance became my motto as I continued my nursing career.

---

"I know, O Lord, that a man's life is not his own; it is not for a man to direct his steps."
*Jeremiah 10:23*

# Chapter 13

## Call to Senior Adult Ministry

"I sought the Lord, and he answered me;
he delivered me from all my fears."
*Psalm 34:4*

Not long after the holidays, I enjoyed an extended visit with my favorite nursing home residents—a delightful married couple. On that breezy afternoon the three of us sat in big green rockers on the front porch at Camellia Gardens.

"Mrs. Griffiths, you're doing a marvelous job. Beulah and I are so pleased you won the 'Employee of the Year' award. You sure deserve it," said Mr. Carlie May.

I asked Mr. May if he would change anything if he could relive his life.

"Well, I always wanted to teach Sunday school, but I never liked talking in front of people," he said. "If I had trusted the good Lord to help me, I could have done it. Just never let shyness keep you from doing what the Lord wants you to do," he added.

His answer was not what I expected. A few months later, Mr. May passed away, but I've never forgotten his wise counsel.

Eighteen months after I became director of nursing at Camellia Gardens, my pastor approached me. "Would you consider teaching the senior adult Sunday school class?" he asked. "I'd also like for you to think about directing the Senior Adult Ministry (SAM). The two go hand-in-hand. Pray about it, Debbie, and let me know what you think."

Clearly someone else could do a far better job. I was puzzled, unable to imagine why my pastor would ask me, still in my twenties, to teach a group of senior ladies and gentlemen. Never before had I taught a Sunday school class, and certainly not the most knowledgeable group in the church.

My anxiety grew just thinking about it.

*The board members recognize your special talent. This would be a great ministry for you and for the church.* His words echoed in my mind whenever I had a moment to myself.

Then I remembered Mr. May's words, and it seemed like more than a coincidence. Nonetheless, that familiar knot settled in the pit of my stomach.

"Why did he ask me to do this?" I asked Bo, looking for a way out.

"Oh, you can do it, Deb. I know you can."

"But Bo, the senior adults know far more about the Bible than I do."

"The Lord will help you," he said. "Just prepare yourself every week."

After several days of prayer, that same feeling settled in—like when I knew the nursing director position was meant for me. I reluctantly trusted that strong feeling, hoping I wasn't making a big mistake.

The minute I arrived at church the following week my pastor confronted me. He wanted an answer.

"I'll take the seniors—the class and the SAM," I said. Even though I felt at peace regarding my decision, doubt still gnawed at my ability to handle the task.

Each Sunday morning I came fully prepared to share the lesson with my "Cumjoynus" class—all over the age of fifty-five. Some Sundays I was nervous as a cat, but without fail, the fear abated after the opening prayer.

Studying the Bible in preparation for my class strengthened me exactly the way Bo had said. It even boosted my confidence as a nursing director.

Serving in a professional management role in conjunction with my church ministry leadership kept me extremely busy, especially after I created a senior adult newsletter—"*SAM SEZ.*" Both the class and the SAM grew by leaps and bounds. One of the highlights of the SAM was the annual senior adult Vacation Bible School with programs and crafts geared especially for seniors.

Over a two-year period, I authored two church-related books inspired by the members of SAM—*Biographies of SAM, Part I and Part II*, detailing a short life history of each senior adult in the church. My aim was to capture the heritage of longtime Thomasville citizens. Church members and local individuals eagerly bought the books. We then used the proceeds to purchase carpet and additional lighting for the senior adult classroom. In spite of Bo's leadership in the Men's Fellowship and Kyle's involvement in extracurricular activities, they were always present at every single event supporting my seniors' ministry.

I remember one Sunday morning when the pastor asked me to come to the front of the church. My heart pounded in my chest as I did as he asked. Much to my surprise, he blessed me with the Sunday school "Teacher of the Year" award. Quite frankly, in the world's eyes, and in mine, I simply couldn't do this. But clearly nothing was impossible for God.

I specifically remember one class member, Mrs. Parrish, a lady I much admired. She suffered macular degeneration and could no longer read the Scriptures; however, she could still recite verses—one right after another—and she did. Her example impacted my life tremendously.

Because many of my Sunday school students, as well as my nursing home residents, had lost their mates, I could easily relate to them; I knew firsthand that gnawing, empty ache that accompanies grief.

Thus far, my life experiences had taught me volumes not only about health and illness but also about living and dying.

---

"The only thing we have to fear is fear itself."
*Franklin D. Roosevelt*

# Chapter 14

## Oncology, This Is Debbie

"I am the Lord your God, who teaches you what is best for you, who directs you in the way you should go."
*Isaiah 48:17b*

One day as I made a quick trip to the local hospital to check on one of my nursing home residents, I nearly collided with my friend Dr. Charlie.

"Hi, Debbie. I was just thinking about you this morning," he said. "The new oncology clinic will open soon, and we'll need a chemo nurse. This would be a great opportunity for you."

"Well, Dr. Charlie, you know I love working with older adults," I responded.

"I understand. I suspect most of the cancer patients would fit that category. With your IV experience and your work there at the nursing home, I believe you would be just the person for the job. I'll submit your name, if that's okay with you."

"Whatever you think."

Bo and I had briefly discussed the possibility of me

working at the cancer center. I thought it curious that I should see Dr. Charlie this morning; the same thing had happened when I was considering the nursing home job.

I wrestled with the thought of leaving my job at the nursing home. For me, it meant leaving my comfort zone. I truly loved the residents. But I was also quite certain that I didn't want to deal with the new regulatory issues Medicaid would require. I finally decided to pursue the oncology center position.

"I'm definitely a people person," I shared with Todd, the hospital recruiter. "I'm very interested in working at the new cancer center, and I have the experience. By the way, Dr. Charlie suggested I talk with you."

During my interview, he informed me that the oncology position would be filled by a hospital employee. "That means you'll need to return to work here, then apply for the position. If you're selected, you will transfer to the chemotherapy department."

Returning to work at the hospital as an IV nurse (a position I had held many years ago) was no easy task for me. The head nurse wasn't happy to see me return, as she believed I had plans to take her job.

One morning I arrived a few minutes early to work. She and I were the only two present in the IV room when out of the blue she started yelling and cursing me. "I know you want my job. Well, just go ahead and take it!"

Not knowing how to respond, I simply replied, "If I wanted to be in a charge position, I would have stayed at the nursing home."

Because of her antagonistic attitude, the next three months were tough. I prayed even more passionately that the oncology center would soon open its doors. Bo encouraged me to keep my chin up and my mind focused. "If the position opens for you, then you'll know it was right."

I was totally unaware that seven other nurses had also applied for the chemo position. *What if they don't select me for the position?* I asked myself. I began to doubt my decision to have left the nursing home.

Week after week I kept to myself, often taking my Sunday school book to work so that during my breaks and at slow times I could study my lesson.

Finally, the long-awaited news came. Julie, the clinical nurse supervisor, had chosen me for the position. "Please report to the new center next Monday morning at 8:30," she wrote in her formal letter.

I remember so clearly the day Julie interviewed me. Because she was just as much a perfectionist as I, we quickly developed a bond. She understood one of my chief reasons for wanting to work in oncology. "I look forward to having the opportunity to make my patients' last days as meaningful as possible," I explained. "It will also allow me the chance to witness—maybe I can make a difference."

Both Julie and I, the first two chemo nurses to work at the center, were nominated as candidates for "Nurse of the Year." Although neither of us won the award, we were honored to have been nominated by an oncology patient.

Every holiday Julie and I dressed in costumes in hopes of making each patient's day brighter. Meanwhile, each weekday after the end-of-day bell rang at Jerger Elementary School, Kyle, now a second-grader, came to visit at the cancer center. While waiting for me to leave work, he increased his circle of friends.

While working at the oncology center, I successfully

obtained certification as a gerontology nurse—satisfying a long-held personal goal.

Julie and I often finished administering treatments to the patients early enough to give us a chance to chat. I remember the Monday I shared with her my Sunday school lesson from the previous day—Genesis 13 and 14. "You know, Julie, God remembered Lot because of Abraham's faith. I pray that He will remember my faith too." Julie understood the burden I felt for my unsaved loved ones and especially my parents.

When my patients (including Uncle Dick, who was one of my cancer patients) got mouth sores, nausea, or diarrhea, so did I! Within a year, I lost twenty-one pounds—pounds I couldn't afford to lose.

I remained in the position at the oncology center until I felt a tug on my heart urging me to seek employment elsewhere. I didn't want to disappoint Dr. Charlie, but I knew he'd understand my predicament.

My patients were not just patients. They had become friends. That included Alesha, a beautiful five-year-old little girl with long blonde hair, blue eyes, and a bubbly personality. After she was diagnosed with leukemia, I administered her chemotherapy. After every treatment she always took my advice and hurried to Arby's for a peach polar swirl—the one icy treat we could both enjoy without experiencing nausea. One year before writing of this book, Bo and I were honored guests at Alesha's beautiful wedding.

---

"There is no such thing in anyone's
life as an unimportant day."
*Alexander Woollcott*

# Chapter 15

## The Mulberry Family

"Commit to the Lord whatever you do,
and your plans will succeed."
*Proverbs 16:3*

Bo and I had just returned from a mission trip to Haiti. The twelve-day reprieve gave me a chance to distance myself from the high level of stress I faced on the job. Although I expected most of my cancer patients to be older adults, it turned out many of them were children—some even babies with brain tumors. This added significantly to my heartache. I genuinely cared about my patients, so much so that I had to find another job for my own well-being.

It was a bright, cheery Monday morning in the chemo clinic. As I sat flanked on the squeaky swivel peach-colored stool, ready to administer my first chemo treatment of the day, the phone rang—right there, in the clinic.

"Excuse me for just a moment please," I said softly to my patient, already reclining in the treatment chair.

The deep, unfamiliar voice on the other end of the phone stated: "Debbie Griffiths, please."

"This is she," I answered.

"Mrs. Griffiths, please accept my apology for calling you at work. Your name was given to me by a lady friend of yours," he said. "She goes to church with you, and she recommended I give you a call. I'd like to talk with you concerning a prospective administrator position—for Mulberry Place. You know, the assisted living facility on Pinetree Boulevard."

"Sir, I'm not really looking for a job," I replied. *Though I probably should be,* I thought but didn't say.

"I understand," he said, "but I'd really like just a few minutes of your time, in person, to discuss this opportunity with you. You received rave reviews from folks in your community concerning your previous work at the nursing home. Also, a family member, whose loved one resides at Mulberry Place, told me your gift is working with the elderly."

I knew it had to be Miss Ann who had given him my name. She was caretaker for Miss Booker, one of the Mulberry residents.

Reluctantly, I accepted his request for an interview, ever mindful of my current job situation. Nevertheless, I wished Miss Ann hadn't given the man my name or my number. I wasn't sure about the new position.

The interview was scheduled the following week, giving me enough time to reflect on the pros and cons of re-entering the field of long-term care. I recognized that I truly missed contact with the residents. The job flexibility was great, but the required on-call duties could be quite demanding. I needed to consider my own health, and I simply could not continue to lose weight as a nurse working in oncology.

My previous experience of nearly five years in a nursing home taught me much about long-term care. At the same time the job had exponentially built my confidence. Still, I wasn't convinced that I'd function well in an administrative capacity. My "stage fright" had decreased, but I still fretted when in front of large crowds, particularly in public presentations that took place outside the comfort zone of my facility.

Several days before the interview, I quietly prayed for a sign so I'd know which direction to take. Driving to the interview, I tried to think of what a good sign might be. I realized most job changes occur as a promotion, so I decided the job opportunity must offer an increase in pay. Even if it was only five dollars more, I would know it was right for me.

When I arrived for the interview, I was amazed at the beauty of Mulberry Place.

I felt good about my interview, but I was certain the pay couldn't possibly exceed my current salary. I established my sign though, knowing only time would tell.

The very next day I received a call—this time at home. "Mrs. Griffiths, my partners and I have talked it over, and we'd like for you to serve as our new administrator. We are willing to pay you an annual salary of twenty-six thousand dollars."

I responded, "Uh ... Sir, I might consider joining your team, but, as an RN, I cannot leave my present job for a pay reduction."

"I understand, Mrs. Griffiths. Think about it, if you will," he suggested.

"I appreciate the phone call," I answered, ready to hang up.

"Hooray," I told Bo. "I knew that job wasn't for me. Now the lady from church will leave me alone and so will the Mulberry partners."

Two nights later, after I had already dismissed the idea of joining the Mulberry team, I received another call from the same gentleman, who said, "Mrs. Griffiths, I talked with my partners again, and we're willing to pay you a salary of twenty-eight thousand dollars. We really want you to be our new administrator."

"Sir, I'm sorry, but as I told you before, I can't leave my current job without a pay increase."

"Would you just think about it and let me know if you change your mind?"

"Yes, I'll think about it," I replied, all the while telling myself that I had established my sign and would not compromise.

I could hardly wait to tell Bo. "Hey, baby, guess what? I know I won't be bothered with this guy anymore. Besides, I've decided I don't want to work at Mulberry Place after all."

"He must not have agreed with your sign," Bo observed. He knew me well.

"Nope, he didn't, and that's it," I said.

The very next evening I was surprised when the same gentleman called me yet again. "Mrs. Griffiths, my company is willing to pay you five hundred dollars more than your current annual salary—whatever that amount is."

This time I knew I was destined to become the new Mulberry Place administrator. For what reason, I didn't know. He had met my sign, but as I told Bo, I wished he hadn't, since I simply didn't want to face any more change.

Mulberry Place was a retirement home—that's basically all I knew. As I riffled through the desk drawers in my new office, I came across a thin yellow licensure booklet. I immediately began acquainting myself with the state rules and regulations. I quickly discovered the facility was licensed as a personal care home. Exactly what that meant, I wasn't absolutely sure. I set about reading every textbook I could find on the subject of *assisted living*.

After reviewing the regulations, I quickly recognized that the facility was nowhere near up to par. It looked beautiful, but behind the scenes, things were not what they seemed. I was determined to make things right.

When I accepted the position, I had no idea the facility was in serious financial trouble. Although Mulberry had been open over three years and was licensed as a twenty-four-bed facility, it had never housed more than thirteen residents. Unbeknownst to me, the owners had planned to give the place six more months to make it under my leadership. If the occupancy didn't increase, the owners would close the doors.

My third day at Mulberry Place, I literally begged the vendor to deliver food. That same scenario repeated itself over several days, even weeks, as I sorted through bundles of business mail to find that the company was nearly fifteen thousand dollars delinquent in paying their bills. I started to question: *Lord, where are you?*

Business classes were never a part of my nursing curriculum. But because I had helped Daddy "figure the bills," I strongly believed I could correct the problems.

Besides, Mama had taught me how to shop for groceries: Watch for the Wednesday specials, use vendor coupons, and stock up when you find a bargain.

One day I received a call from the propane gas company. The facility was using an enormous amount of propane. "That was before you came to work there," the office lady informed me. *How could that be?*

In trying to solve the puzzle, I soon discovered that the gas man had repeatedly delivered an extra two hundred gallons to an employee's personal address, charging the gas to the facility.

"Bo, do you mind if I purchase a computer for my office to help me keep a better handle on the finances? I'll make the monthly payments on it," I promised. A month later I purchased a Tandy computer from Radio Shack and placed it in my office at Mulberry Place.

At my initial staff meeting, I presented my first pet peeve: "Too much time is wasted searching for lost things," I told the group. Together we designed a plan to organize the placement of key items.

At the next meeting, I presented my second pet peeve: "Although this house is big, we can't afford to be packrats. Either we use it or we lose it."

Within thirty days my staff and I could put our hands on anything we needed without a search. Even the financial picture looked a little brighter. Because we discovered food and supplies we didn't know we had, we no longer had the expense of duplicate purchases.

It was important that things be done exactly right, just as I'd learned in my childhood.

Night after night I told Bo, "If I'd known all of this, I

would never have left the security of my hospital job." But I had received my sign; that was enough to make me stick it out.

I discovered that the Mulberry family members suspected some internal problems. Occasionally, I'd find a card on my desk that encouraged me:

> *The Lord has given you a "handful" at Mulberry—but praise the Lord, He never gives us more than we can handle. We are grateful for your caring and loving touch, and we are here when you need us. Proverbs 3:5–6.*

Or a note in the mail:

> *I think you are "planted" right where God wants you. So . . . just keep "blooming" and it will be just as Romans 8:28 promises.*

I recall the day the electrician came to replace the ballast in the laundry room. "Your residents really love you," he said. "They just want to be where you are." Without my knowledge, he had been watching our interactions.

"I love what I do," I told him.

"I can see that."

I remember the first time I called one of the partners about a faulty piece of kitchen equipment. Because the stove was leaking gas fumes, the gas company instructed me not to use the appliance to prepare the evening meal. Rather than cook, my boss told me to purchase hot freshly prepared food from a nearby restaurant for the residents.

His next comment blew my mind: "After all, Debbie, Mulberry is a million-dollar business and the residents deserve the best." That incident alone proved my inexperience; I hadn't grasped the value of the facility I was managing. Each day I learned more about the business and its operations.

Mulberry became the focus of all our energies as a family. Bo, Kyle, and I actually spent every holiday with our "Mulberry family." The highlight of every Fourth of July occurred when Bo barbequed a hog for the residents while Kyle and Mama helped me with the activities.

Kyle's exposure to seniors had begun at Camellia Gardens, where, as a toddler, he sold warm and loving hugs for a quarter to benefit the American Heart Association. He later became my youngest and most loyal Mulberry volunteer. What a gift he was to me and to the residents.

During social hours, Kyle happily conducted impromptu show-and-tell for our residents. They absolutely loved those occasions.

Soon after my arrival at Mulberry, Kyle bonded with his favorite "grandpa," Mr. Beaman. Anytime I needed him, I knew exactly where to find him—in the library playing chess with Mr. Beaman, who had taught him the game. Working with me, Kyle learned to love and to respect older adults.

During our Mulberry days, Mama contributed her time to help me compile our very first cookbook, *Mulberry Munchies*. She and I also scoured the post-holiday department store sales for bargains, always planning ahead for the following year's special events. The Mulberry family had truly become our second family.

One day one of my bosses wrote a lovely tribute: *Activity is Debbie's middle name.* As it turned out, he was the one responsible for me winning the "Administrator of the Year" award in the mid-nineties.

Many evenings after Bo got off from UPS, he came straight to Mulberry Place, where he often worked in the yard or handled repairs without compensation. My family and I worked the business as though we owned it—Mulberry Place became our "home away from home."

Five months to the very day I started, Mulberry Place's occupancy grew from thirteen to a full house—eleven new residents. The owners, the staff, and I were ecstatic. Word spread. Within three months, Mulberry Place had a waiting list!

One afternoon I heard an awful report on the six o'clock news. The reporter asked, "What happens when a home for the elderly is suddenly closed and the residents are forced to leave 'home sweet home' overnight?" My heart instantly broke at their plight. We couldn't believe that situation could occur in a neighboring county. Bo, Kyle, and I abruptly left our home and rescued four residents, using Mulberry's library as temporary housing.

I suggested to the owners the idea of an expansion. Six months later, eleven new suites opened with one hundred percent occupancy. I'm blessed to say the facility never experienced another vacancy during my tenure.

I found that I loved building and construction as well as interior design, which gave me another reason to get excited about geriatric nursing.

Several months later, we built a sister facility fifty miles away. "We want you to help," my boss told me. "What changes need to be made from the original design? Would you handle the inside décor?" he asked, picking my brain.

"You bet I will."

"How much are they going to pay you?" Bo asked. "What about traveling expenses?"

"I didn't think to ask." It really didn't matter to me. Everything was in order at Mulberry. I loved my work, and I relished the new challenge.

Two years later my heart was deeply saddened: "Debbie, the partners and I have decided to sell Mulberry Place," my boss told me. "This is the perfect time to sell."

"Oh no," I said tearfully. My bosses had become like brothers to me, ideal employers. "Please don't sell Mulberry Place," I pleaded. "But if you must, let me buy it."

"Make us an offer."

One week later Bo and I presented our offer to one of the partners: one million dollars!

*Where will the money come from?* If the partners accepted our offer, we had decided we would take the risk.

In the meantime, another one of the owners received a great offer from a huge conglomerate—for double that amount.

Bo and I felt strongly that their offer was excessive. I knew the building better than anyone else, and it would require many expensive changes for the facility to become more senior-friendly. In the first place, the original twenty-four units had all tubs with no walk-in showers. The kitchen freezer and storage areas were terribly inadequate. The list went on. I imagined the upgrades costing a fortune. Nevertheless, it was out of our hands.

The announcement was finally made by the buyers: Mulberry Place would be purchased through the sale of tax-exempt bonds made available through the local

Payroll Development Authority. With my limited business knowledge, I had no idea what was really taking place other than the fact that Mulberry Place was being sold. I did not realize that I could have purchased some of the bonds. No one in management or ownership at Mulberry Place spoke to me about the opportunity. Several local parties who were interested in purchasing bonds called me at Mulberry. "Do you plan to remain as administrator?" they asked.

Each time my reply remained the same: "Don't make your purchase based on my presence. I am not privy to the buyer's future operating plans."

Five days before the sale was final, the buyers called. My position was intact; however, a salary reduction was part of their plan. My immediate response was clear: "Unless my pay stays the same, I cannot accept your offer of employment." Fortunately, the company met my pay requirements, and I was happy as a lark. My desire was to remain a part of the Mulberry family—or so I thought.

Ten months later the facility was sold.

I could never have left Mulberry Place without feeling disloyal to my wonderful bosses. With the facility sold to new owners, I felt better about taking a giant leap of faith to live my dream.

Ten years earlier, I remember sharing with Earl, the physical therapist at Camellia Gardens, my ultimate dream: "Someday I plan to build my own retirement home." Since I had accepted the call to long-term care, I had yearned for the day of owning my own facility. My dream continued to take shape in my mind's eye.

During the sale of Mulberry Place, I shared my vision

with one of the owners. His reply was straight and to the point. It hit me like punch in the midsection.

"Well, Debbie," he said, "many people dream about owning their own facility, but few are able to finance it."

*If others can get the money, so can I,* I vowed to myself. A fiery determination emerged. *Is this business sale happening for a reason? Is his comment the key to motivate me toward my goal?*

From the day I was told Mulberry Place was for sale, the passion to start my own business increased daily. At that point, I had a serious question to answer: *Do I really have what it takes to follow my dream?*

---

"Don't be afraid of the space between your dreams and reality. If you can dream it, you can make it so."
*Belva Davis*

## The *Mulberry* Kitchen Kut-Ups

It's impossible to share my story without introducing my dear friend Miss Lucille, an adorable and energetic woman. She was a legally blind, nearly deaf lady who became a female entrepreneur at age ninety-three—while living in my retirement community. She founded the Kitchen Kut-Ups Band!

It wasn't my idea. I take no credit for it. However, the publicity we gained from her "world-renowned" band frequently put Mulberry and us in the spotlight.

Miss Lucille coyly recruited me as her assistant. We gathered kitchen utensils to serve as makeshift instruments: one grater, two spatulas, four pie plates, a pot lid with a wood spoon, whisk and pancake turner, washboard, small refrigerator rack, set of different size measuring cups, eggbeater, rolling pin, and an empty ice cream bucket with a wooden spoon.

Miss Lucille had become a Mulberry resident shortly after I became administrator. "I'm a music therapist," she had said the moment she introduced herself to me. "Music is one of the greatest medicines ever invented, and because everyone here is old or getting older, we need something to do."

The musical group consisted of sixteen Mulberry residents—ages seventy-four to ninety-six. Some were hearing impaired, while others could scarcely see. Still others used walkers to get around, but none of that mattered. This curious group of musicians lifted the spirits of everyone who heard them play.

"The band uses everything but the kitchen sink to make music." That was the line I used when soliciting band gigs for the Kut-Ups. From Chamber of Commerce meetings to the grand opening of a Kmart store to the *Good Morning Show*, the Kut-Ups performed on the air, on stage, and on the road. They were widely known throughout south Georgia and north Florida.

I later suggested to Miss Lucille that we adopt a theme song—"Achy Breaky Heart." Of course, she had never heard the song—not at her age. After a quick listen though, the song passed her test. "It's gotta have two-four time."

I served as narrator at the band's various functions. Miss Lucille played the piano. She dictated programs and selected songs she had memorized. One band member, Miss Eloise, played her walker using a whisk and a pancake turner to "bring the house down" during the "Achy Breaky Heart" song played from a CD.

I never missed a single one of the 102 performances. Just a few months before I left Mulberry Place, Miss Lucille went home to be with the Lord, but the Kut-Ups continued to play just as she would have wanted.

The business Miss Lucille founded didn't make money, but it added far more than greenbacks. It filled her last days with happy memories and gave us all a new outlook on life.

---

"Nothing is more beautiful than cheerfulness in an old face."
*Jean Paul Friedrich Ritcher*

# Chapter 16

## The Yellow Envelope

"If you have enough fantasies, you're ready,
in the event something happens."
*Sheila Ballantyne*

It was the day after the Mulberry sale. My employers had always promised they would take care of me. As far as I was concerned, they had. They paid me well during the five years I served as administrator. Even though I didn't have a good benefit package, I wasn't too worried. Bo's employment package with UPS met our family insurance needs and would hopefully provide an excellent retirement someday.

Though very little had actually changed overnight, somehow things seemed different at work. I soon realized it was my perception, especially since the new owners were hundreds of miles away. I was already missing my former employers, who had allowed me to manage Mulberry Place as if it was my own. My greatest concern was that my freedom would end.

As I sat at my desk pondering old times, I remembered

a special Christmas party three years earlier that had been held at the Homecoming Restaurant. The facility's owners joined me in honoring the employees with a night of great musical entertainment, door prizes, and Christmas bonuses. I chuckled as I recalled the gag gifts my staff and I had conjured up to give our bosses.

Then I remembered the personal satisfaction I gained while overseeing Mulberry's expansion as well as assisting with its sister facility. Anytime I reflected on the building projects, the thought of designing and operating my own retirement facility was always uppermost in my mind.

At eleven a.m. my office phone rang. I was quickly brought back to earth.

"Debbie, what time are you leaving work today?" the gentleman asked. I knew that familiar voice; it was one of my former bosses.

"I should be off by five p.m.," I answered.

"Would you mind meeting me at Hardees in Quitman?" he asked. "That'll be the halfway point for both of us. The partners have something we want to give you."

That day ended like every other day as I left the building. "See y'all tomorrow everybody. Have a good evening," I said, waving good-bye to the residents and staff as I hurried out the front door.

A quick phone call to Bo alerted him to my plans. He was still delivering in Seminole County, so chances were I'd be home before he arrived. I hurriedly phoned Mama and asked her to pick up Kyle at the soccer field. "As soon as I get back, I'll meet y'all to eat," I suggested.

At precisely 5:30, I drove in the Hardees parking lot, where my former boss sat in his pick-up along with his youngest son. The two immediately got out of the truck and walked toward my vehicle. He was holding a large yellow envelope with my name written in bold black ink on the front. My heart raced.

He greeted me with a smile and a warm handshake. "Thank you for taking time to meet me. I have something for you. It's a small token of our appreciation." With that being said, I carefully opened that envelope. Silently I read the words:

> *Dear Debbie,*
>
> *All of us want to thank you for your efforts above and beyond what was required for your job as administrator of Mulberry Place. We wish you luck in your employment with the new company, who, as of today, has one of the best managers of any personal care home in the country. The three of us wish to give you the enclosed check—not for what you did at work for us—but for what you did for the residents and families of Mulberry Place as well as for the community of Thomasville.*

At that moment I could hardly grasp that the fifty thousand-dollar check had been made payable to me. Tears filled my eyes. I genuinely appreciated the money, but the words on the paper meant far more to me than any cash reward.

"Thank you from the bottom of my heart," I said. "The feelings of gratitude are mutual. I hope and pray our paths will cross again."

As I got back in my car and headed down Highway 84, the tears began to flow. I pulled out a tissue and tried to brush them away, but I couldn't, and for a time, I could hardly see to drive.

As I traveled the highway on that February afternoon, I was immediately reminded of the commitment Bo and I had made to each other the previous year. We had vowed to faithfully tithe to our local church. That year was the first one in our fifteen years of marriage that we had not missed paying a single tithe. I remembered the very last week of that year when I almost talked myself out of writing the check. Paying hefty child support in addition to enormous doctor and dental bills while handling our own living expenses was not easy. In fact, saving was a futile struggle.

While driving, I recalled two Scriptures:

> Give and it will be given to you. A good measure, pressed down, shaken together and running over, will be poured into your lap. For with the measure you use, it will be measured to you.
>
> Luke 6:38

> Bring the whole tithe into the storehouse, that there may be food in my house. Test me in this and see if I will not throw open the floodgates of heaven, and pour out so much blessing that you will not have room for it.
>
> Malachi 3:10

I wondered if the yellow envelope was the reward for obedience.

I was flabbergasted at the mere thought of my employers being so appreciative of me. They were in no way obligated to do it. Then I recalled the bosses' words from the very beginning: "We'll take care of you, Debbie." I knew the gift came from their hearts, and I could hardly wait to share the good news with Bo. Fifteen miles down the road, I grabbed my cell phone from my purse and phoned Bo, sharing the good news. He was as surprised and as pleased as I.

The next morning I awoke before the alarm clock. Holding that check overnight made me extremely nervous; I was eager to get it to the bank. After all, I'd never even seen that much money before in my life.

While sitting in my car in the parking lot waiting for the bank to open, I quietly praised God for allowing me the unique opportunity to work with an employer who genuinely cared about me.

Just as I entered the bank, the thought hit me. I didn't know what to do with the money. I went straight to my banker and asked for his advice.

"If I were you, I'd place it in a passbook savings for now," he said. "With your emotions so high, it's best not to make a rash decision. Besides, you'll have a better feeling later of what you want to do with it."

As I sat at the customer service desk completing the necessary paperwork, tears welled again in my eyes. I would never forget this day as long as I lived.

---

"From what we get, we can make a living;
what we give, however, makes a life."
*Arthur Ashe*

# Chapter 17

## The Toughest Choice

"To live on purpose, follow your
heart and live your dreams."
*Marcia Wieder*

Within the two weeks after Mulberry's sale, I became accustomed to the idea of a new company and new bosses. The management personnel were kind. I was in my comfort zone, and I seriously wanted to remain a part of the Mulberry family.

Bo and I were grateful to have our heads above water financially for the first time in a very long time. We were blessed with the fifty grand in the bank, until April fifteenth, that is. Although we accepted full responsibility for the sixteen thousand-dollar income tax debt, it felt good holding the cash—for a little while anyway.

Meanwhile, Mulberry Place remained fully occupied. The residents and staff hardly recognized any difference after the changeover. I continued to manage the property just as I always had. The biggest difference was the corporate paperwork. I realized it would take time for me to accustom myself to the new way of doing things. Working for a privately owned business had spoiled me.

My days were calm and busy, but my nights were fitful as I wrestled with a tough choice. My dream vied for attention, so the question was: Stay at Mulberry Place or build Southern Pines?

One night in the wee hours of the morning I awakened. I got up, went to the refrigerator, and pulled out a Diet Coke. With my favorite drink in hand, I settled into my favorite mauve wingback chair in the living room. There I began finalizing my plans. I had made up my mind.

I eagerly awaited the sound of the alarm clock. The minute Bo crawled out of bed I greeted him, smiling shyly. "I've decided to build Southern Pines Retirement Inn."

"Whatever you want to do is okay with me," he said. "I'll support you."

I was positive this decision was right—so sure that I ended up bringing home all my personal files. My college class notes as well as other important materials I had created were now placed in a file cabinet in my home for easy and ready reference.

"Where are you planning to store all these files?" Bo asked.

"We'll make a place in the storage room, under the carport."

"What about your computer?"

"No problem. It'll need to stay at Mulberry until the last minute, but then I'll bring it home."

The next week a feeling of sadness settled over me like a dark cloud. I can't possibly leave," I told Bo. "It's my Mulberry family. Can you please help me take the files back to my office?"

The closer I got to my million-dollar dream, the more skeptical I became. This scenario went on for three solid months: back and forth—taking my personal belongings to work and then bringing them back home. One day I planned to build and the next day I gave up the idea altogether.

Then one Thursday night, as I watched Dr. Ronnie Floyd on television, his message penetrated my heart. "What is it that God wants you to do that you are fighting against?" I knew He was speaking to me.

I quickly picked up the phone in my bedroom and called my friend Gwen, who had worked with me for the past nine years at both Camellia Gardens and at Mulberry Place. It didn't matter that it was eleven p.m. She was my friend, and I knew I could share my deepest thoughts with her. As she listened to me share Dr. Floyd's words, I felt her verbal nudge. "Thomasville needs another retirement home. Don't forget you have twenty-one people on the waiting list, and no one is more qualified than you to build a facility." I knew then I had to build.

The next day my feelings vacillated again. Mulberry Place provides me an excellent salary. *I'm scared. I can't do this. Why in the world would I leave a position of comfort to take such a risk?*

Finally, the night came when the passion was more than I could ignore. As Bo and I lay cuddled in bed, his head nestled against mine, he could sense my turmoil. For the umpteenth time, we discussed the possibility of building Southern Pines. "I wish God would send me a sign from heaven right now," I said with a sigh. "Then I'd know for sure the right decision."

"Deb, do you remember the story—the one about the man and the helicopter?"

"I'm not sure what story you're talking about. Tell me about it."

"A man was on his rooftop during a flood when he prayed for the Lord to rescue him. Shortly, a helicopter, a small boat, and a raft all came by as the man patiently proclaimed he was waiting on the Lord. After he drowned, he asked Saint Peter why he was abandoned after so much prayer. Saint Peter told him the Lord had sent him a helicopter, a boat, and a raft for his rescue. But sadly, the man was waiting for something more spectacular.

"Deb, has it occurred to you that the yellow envelope is the helicopter?" he asked. "The nudge from Gwen is likely the boat. And our discussion tonight is the raft. Maybe that's why you are struggling with your decision so much," he said.

A few minutes later Bo was fast asleep while I lay wide awake feeling restless. I eased out of bed and headed to my chair. This time I was making bigger plans. There was no doubt I *had* to follow my dream.

The following week Bo took a day off from UPS. Together we met with our bank friend. "Debbie, I'm not the least bit surprised you're here today," he told me. "In fact, if you don't build your own place, I'll be mighty surprised," he added. "I have no reservations regarding the success of your business."

*Gee, even my banker thinks I should pursue my dream.*

When my banker suggested I hire an accountant, I remembered a gentleman who participated in our Bald Head Recognition Day at Mulberry Place. When I mentioned his name, my banker knew him and agreed that he would be a good choice. Within minutes the accountant was sitting in the bank with the three of us. "I am more than happy to help you with this project, Debbie. Here is a list of items I'll need. Let's meet at my office in a month or so," he confirmed. "That'll give you a chance to get everything together."

From that day forward, I never once looked back. I didn't have the slightest idea of what was ahead of me, but I made a purposeful decision to face every obstacle as an opportunity. Southern Pines Retirement Inn was definitely my dream, and I intended to see it to fruition.

After that initial meeting, I no longer felt the need for Bo to take off work to be with me. I was comfortable, ready to do the leg work—all by myself.

The next week I met with an attorney, just as my banker had suggested. His first suggestion was for me to resign from my current position at Mulberry Place. I hated to hear his suggestion, though I knew he was right. There was no way I could work full-time and give my dream my best effort.

"Bo, the attorney said for me to quit my job, but he doesn't understand. I can't just leave my people," I said.

"Deb, you need to listen … and do what he tells you."

As with all of my duties, I responded to each task with a sense of urgency. At 9:30 p.m., I slipped into my office, hoping to spend time alone. As I sat down at my desk and stared at my computer, tears began to stream down my face. Writing a letter of resignation from Mulberry Place was a task I had never anticipated.

Regardless of my fickle feelings, my attorney had made it clear that leaving my current job was mandatory. "It'll take every bit of twelve hours a day to start a business like this," he had cautioned me more than once.

The next day I nervously submitted my letter of resignation to the corporate office. Then the thirty-day countdown began.

During my final days at Mulberry Place, I spent every free moment after work roaming the city, looking for the perfect land on which to build. Kyle, Mama, and occasionally Gwen rode with me. Because Bo seldom arrived home before eight o'clock, I had plenty of time to search in the daylight.

One day as I was headed to work, I noticed a "For Sale" sign. It was advertising an eleven-acre tract of land on the opposite side of the road positioned diagonally from Mulberry Place. With the owner's permission, that afternoon we drove through the property.

Three days before my final day at Mulberry, Bo asked a thought-provoking question, one I hadn't considered. "When you find the land, how do you plan to pay for it?" I learned quickly that every business venture requires a devil's advocate.

Without the slightest hesitation, I replied, "I don't really know. But when I find the land, I'll figure it out." He always shook his head in wonderment at my lack of concern. By this time, my passion definitely exceeded my doubt.

Bo's response was simple. "Remember, Deb, the fifty grand will soon become thirty-four thousand dollars. And that's not a drop in the bucket compared to the price of land."

"I know... We'll just have to wait and see."

I didn't discuss my plans with my new boss at Mulberry

Place until the last two weeks. Then he offered to try to find some of the tax-exempt bonds for me to purchase.

"That way you'll feel a part of the ownership of Mulberry Place," he said. "You won't need to build a place then."

"I've made my decision. I'm building Southern Pines." After a pause, I explained further. "My hometown needs a second personal care home. The facilities will compliment one another. They will both be successful."

For four months I had diligently worked with the new owners to facilitate the transition. Yet everyday I struggled with my own passion.

On the night of June 14, the eve of my last day at Mulberry, my church friend Ann joined with the Mulberry residents and staff to host a most memorable going-away party. The lovely dining room was filled with residents, staff, and family members who came to say good-bye and wish me well as I started on the road to entrepreneurship. Tears of joy mixed with tears of sadness. I was already missing my extended family.

But I knew I had to leave. Only in leaving could I take my dream to reality.

---

"To be courageous means to be afraid, but  
to go a little step forward anyway."  
*Beverly Smith*

# Chapter 18

## Location, Location, Location

"I will love the light for it shows me the way. Yet I will endure the darkness for it shows me the stars."
*Og Mandino*

Now that my responsibilities at Mulberry Place were complete, it was time for me to get busy. I made a mad dash to see Mr. Nat. I couldn't get that eleven-acre parcel of land off my mind. The possible purchase resulted in a series of three serious negotiations.

Mr. Nat had already contracted for the removal of a large number of gorgeous pine trees from the property. I sadly watched as the trees were hauled off one by one. I had placed a contingency in the purchase document, allowing me a second look at the land once the trees were cut down. I was sick. It wouldn't work at all. So, after vetoing the plan, I had to begin my search all over again.

Although I thought the land within shouting distance of Mulberry Place was a prime location for Southern Pines, Mama and Bo disagreed. They realized I was having trouble leaving my first love. I finally accepted the fact that building near Mulberry was not such a good idea after all.

One afternoon during my daily search, I discovered a second parcel of land located on East Pinetree, close to town. The real estate agent informed me there was no city sewage available in the area. With twenty-six toilets in the plans for Southern Pines, the land obviously was not a feasible option. The agent agreed to check the cost for sewage to be added if I wanted, but I certainly couldn't wait for that to happen.

One day as I traveled from one side of town to the other, I zipped down Covington Avenue, a side street. As I made the shortcut that day, I noticed a sign laying on the ground. It looked like it had fallen off a post. I hit the brakes and jumped out to read the script on the sign: *Three or more acres for sale. For more information, call…*

It sounded like a viable option to me. *Wow! What a location*! I thought to myself. It appeared to be an optimum building site in every way. I immediately called Bo to tell him of my find. I was certain the land wouldn't last long, and I wanted Bo to come by that very evening to give me his opinion.

I could see from the looks of the handwritten sign that no realtor was involved. That would save some dollars. I established the maximum cost I could spend for land. "I sure hope it's in my budget," I told Bo.

"Now where did you say the land was located?" he asked.

"On Covington Avenue, you know, where the new Rose Garden has just been located… "

"You don't mean it?"

"Yes, I do!"

"I'll get home as soon as I can, and we'll go look at it together."

With an exact dollar figure in mind, I made an appointment to meet Mr. Wade, the owner of the property with the misplaced sign. He and I met on the back screened porch overlooking Puzzle Lake. I enjoyed the view of his gorgeous mallard ducks and geese, and we soon became acquainted.

His sweet wife, Jessie, came out of the house when I first arrived, but smiled as she quickly made her way back inside, leaving Mr. Wade alone to handle the business at hand. I was glad to have met her.

"How much land do you need?" he asked me.

"Well, sir, I could get by with two acres—especially since I don't have much money right now." *I don't have any money, actually,* I thought. *But if he'll sell me the land, I'll find the money,* I told myself. "I saw on your sign that you were advertising three acres or more. How much total land is there?"

"Oh, I'd say there are about twenty-five or so acres."

"Will you *please* consider selling me only two acres?"

"What are you planning to build on the property?" he inquired.

"A lovely retirement home with twenty-four spacious suites for seniors," I said. "You've probably heard of it before—it's called assisted living. Some people call them personal care homes." I explained. "Then in a year or so I'll add another twelve suites—but I really have to start small, Mr. Wade."

As he sat in his rocking chair, staring at two colorful geese that slowly made their way into view, I knew he was pondering the idea of a two-acre sale. My heart pounded as I awaited his response.

"Well, little lady, I suggest you go ahead and buy the three acres. I have a feeling if you buy the acreage and build the home, the people will come."

"But Mr. Wade, I'm not sure I can afford three acres right now. How much do you want for the three acres of land?"

"Let's get in my old Lincoln out front there, little lady, and I'll drive you through the Oak Grove property, originally a landscape nursery, so you can get a real good look at the land. It's beautiful, and it's a good place to build."

"Okay, Mr. Wade, I'm ready. Let's go."

"Let me think about the price," he said after we had completed the tour.

Two days passed and still Mr. Wade hadn't given me a firm price on the land.

"Please, Mr. Wade, I need to know now how much you want for the land."

"Well, little lady, I've been thinking about it. I'd love to see a retirement facility on my old homeplace property. I know Jessie is going to need it."

Having recently learned Mr. Wade was eighty-one years old, I struggled to keep a straight face.

"Yes, Mr. Wade, I understand. If we live long enough, all of us will eventually need some help. You know what they say," I added, "don't regret growing old—it's a privilege denied to many."

The following day, Mr. Wade called with his answer. "Well, little lady, I'll sell you three acres for $110,000."

"But Mr. Wade, my land budget can only afford one hundred thousand dollars. If you'll sell me just two acres,

I'm sure I'll buy another acre in a year or two. Or I'm willing to pay $37,500 for each acre. But I just can't go way over my budget like that. Do you understand, Mr. Wade?"

"Little lady, listen to what I'm telling you—if you'll build the suites, the residents will come," he reminded me again.

"Mr. Wade, would you consider splitting the price down the middle? I'm willing to go over budget five thousand dollars if you are willing to drop the price five thousand dollars," I negotiated. "If you'll agree to sell me three acres for $105,000, then you got yourself a deal—today."

"You will need those three acres, little lady," he said. "You need to build fifty spaces because twenty-four simply aren't enough." Then he asked, "When do you want to close the deal?"

"As soon as possible," I said eagerly. "Uh, give me two weeks, Mr. Wade. You go ahead and get your ducks in a row, because I'll be ready real soon."

I couldn't get home fast enough to share the exciting news with Bo.

"By the way, where are you going to get the money to buy the land?" Bo asked. I remembered that same question surfacing a few weeks ago.

"I don't know, but I'll get it," I replied. "You can bet on that!"

"Remember what you told me," he said.

"Oh, yes, no need to worry, Bo," I answered. "I'll definitely hold the majority ownership. Bo, I'm so excited. Soon my project will be underway. Today I'm planning to find some money."

"Just be careful where you get it," he cautioned.

"Don't worry, baby. I want investors who have the same morals we do."

---

"Some people succeed because they are destined to, but most people succeed because they are determined to."
*Anonymous*

# Chapter 19

## Start-up Ain't Easy

"You are not given a dream, without being given the power to make it come true."
*Anonymous*

*Retirees Wanted!* That was the headline on the front page of the local newspaper one month after my Mulberry resignation. Word was out… A new locally owned retirement community was on its way.

The very first sentence of the news article read: *Former Mulberry Place administrator Debbie Griffiths will open a licensed retirement home in February.* The media's method of alerting our town prompted a disparaging rumor. The last thing I wanted was for it to seem that I was planning to be in competition with my beloved Mulberry Place. After all, it was part of who I was.

Those who knew me had heard me share my dream many times. They would know better than to believe the rumors. Yet for the first time, I realized business ownership required a thick skin. I prayed I'd be prepared to meet the ownership role head-on.

Since I was now unemployed, Bo and I pictured our own finances without my paycheck. We learned fast that sacrifice was the name of the game when it came to establishing one's own business.

A year or so before, we consolidated two vehicle loans as well as a small charge card balance to create a second mortgage on our home. The balance of the second mortgage totaled nine thousand dollars. We paid the debt in full from the thirty-four thousand dollars left, after taxes. We had a mere balance of twenty-five thousand dollars to our name—still more than we ever had before.

While browsing the local newspaper, I stumbled across an opportunity—a training session sponsored by the Small Business Administration and the local Chamber of Commerce. The all-day class taught me a great deal about the dos and don'ts of starting a business. I felt grateful for the new knowledge.

At the end of the session, I eagerly awaited my chance to meet one-on-one with the instructor. I excitedly described my prodigious Southern Pines plans. "I just relinquished an excellent paying job to pursue my dream," I told him. "It'll be hard, but my husband and I are willing to sacrifice." He understood time was crucial in bringing my dream to life, especially since I no longer received a paycheck.

While reviewing the bank's checklist of required documents, he suggested I budget a small monthly salary for myself during the start-up phase. "You should at least pay yourself something. Start-up is not an easy job," he cautioned me. This was just one of many tips I learned while on the road to small business ownership.

My accountant and I called it the numbers game. My

job was to detail the cost of every single item I needed for Southern Pines, from paper clips to furniture to equipment. "The numbers must work," he reminded me, "or your dream cannot become a reality."

*The numbers will work,* I told myself. *I will find prices that fit in my budget.* I was determined to make it work.

Each potential vendor offered a written proposal, which I collected in a three-ring binder. With all the paperwork completed, my business plan easily measured six inches thick. Within thirty days, I was ready to review the numbers with my accountant.

I had played the numbers game long enough to know that a million-dollar loan was necessary to finance my dream. My accountant told me the bank required twenty-percent working capital before lending a million dollars. I would need two hundred thousand dollars just to open the account.

My next daunting task was to find the honest and reputable investors Bo and I had discussed. The managing partner of the law firm, who set up my limited liability company, volunteered his group as part of my team. *Even my attorneys approve of my dream,* I thought with excitement. They willingly wrote an $85,000 check for nineteen percent ownership.

Then I thought about the wonderful group of pharmacists I had worked with through the years at Camellia Gardens and Mulberry Place. After discussing my plan, they happily agreed to invest $85,000 for nineteen percent ownership.

With our twenty-five thousand dollars, I felt fairly comfortable asking the banker to allow me to start with $195,000 cash. Besides, the $170,000 was raised in just seventy-two hours. I was sure my banker would be impressed.

Shortly before I planned to meet with the banker, my accountant phoned. After careful consideration, he had decided I needed another fifty-five thousand dollars to get started. Suddenly, my heart sank.

"Are you absolutely sure?"

"Yes, then you can pay for the land from the working capital and use it as collateral. That'll leave you close to $150,000 to start," he said. "I'll feel better if you begin with $250,000 total."

"Whatever you say, sir … I'm depending on you."

At that moment, the name of a physician came to mind. I had made rounds with him at the nursing home for years, and I was hopeful that he would come through for me. I wanted him to view the projections I held in my hands.

Without studying my proposal, he immediately shot me down. "Debbie, you're going to fall on your face. Have you lost your mind? You don't understand depreciation or taxes. Besides, Thomasville doesn't need another facility. You'd better think twice!"

Although I was in a state of shock, I replied, "Doc, I really appreciate your concern. Obviously what you don't understand is this—I'd rather try and fail than to regret never having tried." Although my decision was firm, by the time I hung up doubt had again reared its ugly head. I couldn't believe he would try to dissuade me from following my dream when everyone else was behind me.

Then a new thought hit me. My mom's boss, Mr. Len, was like a brother. He was mindful of my previous business experience. With no doubts, he graciously handed me a check for $55,000, for eleven percent interest in my dream, adding that he considered it a privilege to join my investment group. I promised to make him proud.

A top-notch and highly reputable investment team was now in place—all of whom were males. But having all male investors turned out to be a wonderful blessing; they didn't care what color paint I chose or what type dinnerware I selected. In less than a week, I deposited $250,000 into the new Southern Pines bank account.

However, I remembered a very important word of advice from a loyal and dedicated friend—my former boss. "Since you are the expert in this business, Debbie, make sure you *always* remain the majority owner." I never forgot his wise counsel.

The Covington Avenue building site was now under contract. Successfully raising the funds to pay off the land confirmed that my dream would shortly be reality. Unfortunately, I was still five thousand dollars over budget, which caused some anxiety, but I decided I would find another way to make up the deficit.

I knew I could save by designing the interior myself, sticking to my business plan down to the last detail. And that became my game plan—to do as much of the work myself as I could and stay within the confines of my set budget. The only flexibility I allowed myself was to pull from one budget line item to another.

Through my previous experience in design, I had gleaned valuable insight into design ideas that would facilitate resident care. Working hand in hand with my architect, I replaced bathtubs with showers and increased the size of the suites to accommodate wheelchairs and walkers. I also planned to add elegant accent colors to cheer up the common areas of my dream community.

I wanted to get started building right away, which meant searching for the right construction company to build Southern Pines. With eight sets of architectural plans in hand, I distributed invitations to bid. The construction industry was very busy, so only three of the bids were returned.

I became excited when one proposal came in from a highly reputable company in neighboring Mitchell County. The project manager, Jamie, and I walked the land and, using bright orange tape, we roped the exact location of where Southern Pines was to sit on the property.

It wasn't long before it was time for the groundbreaking ceremony. Eight speakers made brief opening remarks—everyone from the mayor to the land owner to our wonderful twelve-year-old son. Their encouragement touched me as a new business owner, but the words that touched me the most came from Kyle: "My dad and I will be Mom's greatest supporters."

The day ended on a special note when children from the daycare center next door sang an adorable and rousing chorus of "Jesus Loves Me."

I remember the excitement I felt the day Bo and Kyle erected the sign on the building site: *Southern Pines Retirement Inn—Coming Soon!* One glance at the old, faded four-by-eight plywood sign, now stored in our barn, continues to remind me of the satisfaction I still feel today.

I felt a similar emotion the day Jamie ordered delivery of a twelve-foot job site trailer for me. That became my "office" where I wrote policies and procedures, the employee handbook, filed applications for licensure, and hired my original staff. During the Christmas holidays, I proudly decorated my site office and listened to the sounds of holiday tunes playing on my boom box.

I recall the day I peered through that decorated trailer window with tears streaming down my face. From there I watched and supervised Southern Pines' construction—from the ground up. It was hard to believe my dream was unfolding right before my very eyes. A favorite Scripture came to my mind: "If God be for me, then who can be against me?" (Romans 8:31). It was a verse I would meditate on every day of my life as an entrepreneur.

Mulberry's success had been directly related to my former bosses' perspective on management and operations; they never expected me to place the needs of the company ahead of the needs of the residents. That would also be my policy at Southern Pines.

At my very first business meeting, I distributed a handout to each partner. The following words were typed in large print: *Southern Pines will become a spectacular success! We as a partnership must never allow our individual wants to come ahead of the needs of the residents.* Our group adopted that standard from the beginning.

I remembered reading Larry Burkett's book: *Business by the Book–Biblical Guidelines for Men and Women in Business.* My former Mulberry boss—the one who always guided me in my ongoing business decisions—and I had discussed the principles in this book many times. He knew I planned to adhere to Mr. Burkett's valuable advice with high hopes of making Southern Pines a success.

I later learned that another one of my Mulberry bosses speculated that I'd build my dream facility within five years. The three Mulberry partners knew me as a visionary and were not the least bit surprised when they saw the sign: *Southern Pines Retirement Inn—Coming Soon!*

---

"Success comes from doing the best you can do…
pursuing your dreams till you make them come true."
*Anonymous*

# Chapter 20

## Million-Dollar Dream: Southern Pines Retirement Inn

"Courage is doing what you are afraid to do!
There can be no courage unless you're scared."
*Eddie Richenbacker*

I have magnificent dreams—the kind that start small and grow fast in no time. That's exactly what happened when I finally stepped out in faith.

Those who knew me understood my passion. They saw it in my daily walk. If they were around long enough, they heard me talk about it almost incessantly. Those who watched me recognized it wasn't just a fantasy but a burning desire deep down in my soul.

In my head I pictured the inside of the building as well as the beautifully landscaped grounds. In my imagination, I had already named it Southern Pines Retirement Inn. Having the word "Inn" as part of the name reminded me that my residents were really my guests. That's how I expected each one to be treated—with utmost respect and dignity. To me, "Older Americans are our greatest natural resource."

True to my vision, I carefully designed the stately Victorian-style brick home. The interior décor represented the Rose City—my hometown. Each of the five long hallways (streets) I named for the property: Rosebud Court, Magnolia Way, Dogwood Trail, Azalea Bend, and Camellia Crossing. The framed prints and silk arrangements used in the décor complimented the theme of each street.

Seven pictures painted by a local artist hung in the spacious living room—including a picture of the Big Oak, the oldest and largest tree in Thomasville. A beautiful fireplace complete with a white mantle and burgundy accent added to the ambience of the room. A hanging brass chandelier often reflected in the mirror that hung above the mantle. A grandfather clock and a piano were part of the furnishings.

I named the elegant dining room the Tea Room. A gorgeous cherry hutch displayed the china Bo and I selected when we married. The Victorian oval cherry wood tables with Queen Anne legs and upholstered chairs made the Tea Room feel classically comfortable. Teapots above the sparkling white cabinets added a Victorian flair. On every monthly activity calendar, I listed a formal "Tea Time at the Inn."

The exit off Rosebud Court led to the Quail's Nest, a screened sunroom, which housed a gorgeous wood aviary containing a dozen or more cheerful and lively finches. Furnished with green, heavy-weight wrought iron outdoor furniture, it soon became a popular private dining location.

An on-site beauty shop, a library, and a Jacuzzi were made available for relaxation and refreshing.

At the corner of Dogwood Trail and Azalea Bend

sat the Briar Patch, a quaint little gift shop stocked with small gift items and a variety of cards.

Adjacent to Azalea Bend sat the Rose Room—a spacious game room where residents could enjoy movies and games. A separate exercise area adjoined the Rose Room.

A second smaller activity room called the Robin's Nest was situated at the intersection of Azalea Bend and Camellia Crossing. Pine Cove was a bright, cheery sunroom overlooking the Miracle Garden—a lovely butterfly garden, one of two courtyards at Southern Pines. In the center of the garden a pond held fish that Kyle loved to feed.

*The gardens at Southern Pines Retirement Inn*

A covered breezeway, Memory Lane, provided a shortcut from Pine Cove to the Tea Room. In the center of the breezeway a gazebo was made available for rest and relaxation. To the cupola of the gazebo, we welded a wrought iron pinecone, donated by a family in honor of their beloved mother.

An eight-foot-wide outdoor barbeque grill, uniquely designed by Bo, was built during the initial construction and was often used during family gatherings.

Southern Pines Retirement Inn started as my *million-dollar dream. Phase I* consisted of twenty-four spacious suites—twenty standard and four deluxe. Not only was the bathroom in each suite designed with handicap needs in mind, but so were the spacious closets, the lighting, and the appropriate nurse call system.

Southern Pines' location created a unique marketing advantage, as it was situated across the street from the city-owned rose garden with its exquisite display of five hundred roses. Southern Pines' wide front porch overlooked the sparkling waters of the picturesque Cherokee Lake.

During the construction, I watched as many boards were hammered and many bricks were laid. Every single day I made rounds—with Jamie. We both wanted to make sure things were being done right: exactly like the plans showed. I absolutely loved the building phase, especially since it was *my dream* unfolding before my very eyes.

The construction team worked seven days a week. In less than five months, the eighteen-thousand-square-foot dream facility was erected. I was thankful for my past business expertise that made it all possible and such an incredibly satisfying experience.

Shortly after construction began, Jamie kindly informed me that a savings of six thousand dollars was possible by eliminating the crown molding in each of the resident's suites and bathrooms. But that wasn't an option. My vision simply did not include cutting corners.

I wanted my residents to enjoy "Retirement Living at Its Finest." In fact, that catchy phrase became my slogan along with the pinecone logo—all indicative of my amazing Southern Pines.

While the construction team built the physical plant, I selected all the inside furnishings—from kitchen equipment to window treatments. Mama joined me in my travels to the Atlanta gift market and to various furniture showrooms in North Carolina. My favorite part was choosing the furniture fabrics and the accessories.

I could scarcely contain my excitement when, before the foundation was even poured, twenty-four paid reservations were deposited in the bank. When Jamie learned of the one hundred percent occupancy, he immediately notified the construction company owner, Mr. Cameron. He encouraged me to consider building *Phase II*—eleven standard suites and one deluxe. That thought had crossed my mind, but I hadn't planned that phase until two years down the road.

My biggest concern wasn't the possible vacancies, but the additional $650,000 I would need to build the second phase. Mr. Cameron asked for direction as soon as possible—whether to add the walls on the north end of the building or to build the six thousand square-foot addition.

The partnership agreement was clearly spelled out. To build another phase, each partner was responsible for providing a certain percentage of the down payment. My percentage was an awesome thirty thousand dollars.

*Where will I get the money?* I asked myself.

Though I was willing to do just about anything to facilitate the expansion, I hesitated at the idea of mortgaging our private residence or relinquishing any more of my ownership percentage.

I always remembered my former boss's words of advice: "Without fifty-one percent of the stock, you lose your role as primary decision-maker." I had no option. I would keep majority ownership so that I could guarantee my residents excellent quality care. I also wanted to be sure the facility would not be sold until I was good and ready to sell it.

Much to my surprise, I received a phone call from Mr. Cameron. "Debbie, have you gone to the bank to borrow the money?"

"No, Mr. Cameron, I haven't. I plan to go this afternoon."

"Don't worry about your portion of the down payment," he said. "I'll personally loan you the money at a lower interest rate. I'll have my attorney arrange the documents for you to sign tomorrow morning."

An immediate sense of gratitude overwhelmed me. Once more, I quietly thanked God for looking after me.

Nine months from the day I signed the documents for that special loan, I proudly made the seventy-mile round trip to hand-deliver Mr. Cameron a check for the balance of the thirty thousand dollars plus interest on the note. His act of kindness was a huge encouragement.

Jamie said I could schedule occupancy for the first phase on Friday, March 1, 1996. When that morning arrived, the state fire marshal came for the final inspection and discovered a malfunctioning sprinkler head. That meant he was unable to issue a certificate of occupancy. Instantly, I sank into despair. In five months, I had never been the least bit upset, but that day I sat on the vacant floor of the library and cried.

Because four residents were scheduled to move in each day, it was time for some quick thinking. I had a responsible employee, Miss Vera, put off the move-in date three days for each resident. Bo and I later decided my tears of sadness were actually tears of relief. In reality, the delay would allow us another seventy-two hours to move all the furnishings into place before the first residents arrived.

That weekend Miss Vera worked diligently alongside Bo and me. Since she had worked with us the past five years at Mulberry Place, she knew exactly how I wanted things done. While tending to our many tasks, Miss Vera (who often reminded me of my black mama, Miss Lena) and I engaged in one of our heart-to-heart chats.

"Miss Vera, I sure hope Mama will recognize the giant risk I've taken to build Southern Pines. Maybe my faith will serve as a witness to her. I pray she'll come to know the Lord."

"Baby, we just need to pray about it. I had no idea Miss Pauline hadn't accepted the Lord. She's such a wonderful person," Vera commented.

Since *Phase II* was due to open on June 1, I delayed my Grand Opening until both phases were complete.

*Ribbon Cutting at Southern Pines Retirement Inn, Phase I and II*

Three months later, *Phase II* opened as planned. Another twelve residents joined our Southern Pines family—all within three days. The facility was one hundred percent occupied.

Already I begin to envision a third expansion—nine more standard suites and three deluxe. However, I hadn't anticipated a *Phase III.* I never once thought the total number of residents would exceed thirty-six—not now, not ever!

Six months later, on a cool, sunny morning, a nicely dressed gentleman entered my office, located just to the left of the front entrance. It was clear that he had something on his mind.

"Good morning, little lady. I'm looking for Mrs. Griffiths," the handsome fellow stated.

"Sir, I am Mrs. Griffiths. How may I help you?" I asked.

"Well, I wasn't expecting someone as young as you to be Mrs. Griffiths," he said as he shook my hand.

"You do own this place, right?" he questioned.

"Yes, sir, I do."

As he pulled out a sheaf of papers from his briefcase, he continued. "Mrs. Griffiths, I've been recruited by a major retirement chain to present this proposal to you. The company heard about your lovely facility and your excellent track record. They are interested in purchasing Southern Pines. I'd like to discuss this proposal with you."

Although it agitated me, I said softly, "I'm sorry, sir, but I'm not interested. I love what I do. Besides, I'm considering further expansion in the near future."

"Well, aren't you at least interested in hearing about their offer?" he asked. "I have it here in my hand."

"No, sir, I'm really not. But it has certainly been nice meeting you," I said as I rose from my chair.

He immediately stood. "Well, Mrs. Griffiths, uh … I need to alert you."

"Yes, sir, I'm listening."

"The company has asked me to tell you that if you aren't willing to sell, they intend to build a facility here. They want you to be aware that it will create some rather stiff competition for you."

Although his comment caught me off guard, my response was soft and calm. "Well, sir, I suggest you tell the company to proceed with their project. I have utmost confidence that Southern Pines will continue to be successful. It's my ministry, and I believe that as long as I operate Southern Pines with my residents' best interests in mind, we'll be fine."

Less than a year after the opening of *Phase II*, the third phase was in progress. This time the bank didn't require any cash up front. Finally, the equity was there and my business could vouch for itself.

Just as with *Phase I* and *II*, future residents placed the deposits to acquire a suite in the new section. Before construction was completed, Southern Pines was once again one hundred percent occupied.

During this phase of construction, Mr. Wade introduced me to the beautiful pinecone lily. At least twice weekly, he dropped by my office with a pinecone bloom in a large vase. At the grand opening of *Phase III*, he presented a surprise gift of ten pinecone bulbs to add next to the herb garden.

Meanwhile, Daddy, in his own quiet way, slipped in often with a beautiful bouquet of yellow roses from his yard. I'd later find them on the corner of my desk.

After the opening of *Phase II*, Mr. Wade and Mrs. Jessie joined me for lunch often, especially if fried chicken was on the menu. Much of our table talk evolved around Southern Pines.

"Little lady, didn't I tell you from the beginning to build fifty spaces?" he asked as if I'd forgotten our earlier conversation.

"Yes, Mr. Wade, you did. I'll admit, you were right all the time."

"And if you keep building, they'll keep coming," he encouraged.

"Mr. Wade, are you aware that we're getting two new facilities in town?"

"Yeah, I heard about them, but let me tell you something, little lady. With your fine reputation, you have nothing to worry about. Trust me."

"Well, Mr. Wade, I suspect they won't have an RN as director either."

"And neither will they have an owner as director."

"You're right about that, Mr. Wade. It's very uncommon for owners to operate their own facilities. Especially one the size of Southern Pines, but I'll just keep doing my best to take care of my ladies and gentlemen."

"You do that, little lady, and you'll be all right."

The operation, now in its third year, never experienced a single vacancy—not even for one day. My goal was to pay the original twenty-year amortized note in full within fifteen to seventeen years, and it looked like a good possibility.

The personal care home was licensed for fifty-four. That allowed couples or relatives to occupy the same suite. For the first time since opening, my waiting list dwindled from twenty to twelve. Sometimes the potential resident's health didn't allow him to wait for a vacancy at Southern Pines.

For more than a year no major construction took place, except for a small asphalt job, when twenty-eight guest parking spaces were added that summer.

After the completion of *Phase III*, I vowed—no more construction! Overseeing a major building project and handling the usual day-to-day operations turned out to be an exhaustive and massive undertaking. No matter who suggested expansion or how long the waiting list grew, I was bound and determined, I was finished.

---

"Courage is fear that has said its prayers!"
*Ruth Fishel*

## Have Pinecone Band, Will Travel

There was no question in my mind that Southern Pines had to have its own band. It was the perfect way to pay tribute to my former Mulberry resident Miss Lucille. Besides, I'd never forget how much fun the residents and I had entertaining the various audiences. Without a doubt, the band was the highlight of my planned activity program at Mulberry Place.

Within a month after opening, I organized the Pinecone Band. The name felt right, just as did the new pinecone logo. Pinecones represent optimism. Because I knew my goals for the band, the name fit perfectly. The band had its own business cards with miniature pinecones attached to each card by a green silk ribbon. No one ever forgot the Pinecone Band!

The band's earliest members included sixteen of the facility's twenty-four residents, ranging in ages from seventy-two to ninety-six.

Miss Ruth joined the Pinecone Band two years later. As the oldest band member, she made music using the whisk and the pancake turner. But once the "Achy Breaky Heart" song began to play, she put her instruments aside, eased from her seat, and danced to the music. She never missed a chance to raise her leg like a Radio City Music Hall Rockette ready to perform. For eight years she lived with us and never missed a single performance. Audiences were always amazed at her agility, especially at age 106.

*Miss Ruth and Pinecone Band at Kiwanis Meeting*

Like Miss Lucille at Mulberry Place, Miss Ruth blessed my business efforts by standing to give credit at the end of every performance. The publicity alone was invaluable for the reputation of Southern Pines. Two years after I sold the business, Miss Ruth died at Southern Pines—at the ripe old age of 108.

Like the famous Kitchen Kut-Ups of Mulberry Place, the Pinecone Band was always on the go. With their makeshift instruments, they thrilled and stunned audiences. The vivacious group entertained 129 different audiences during my tenure, averaging more than one performance a month. Never did I miss a single performance except during the longest year when my parents became my main focus.

---

"Old age has its pleasure, which, though different,
are not less than the pleasures of youth."
*W. Somerset Maugham*

# Chapter 21

## Multimillion-Dollar Dream: Southern Pines Retirement Community

"Our greatest weakness lies in giving up. The most certain way to succeed is to always try just one more time."
*Thomas Jefferson*

It was midnight. I couldn't sleep, so I climbed out of bed and made my way to my home office—a four-by-seven room adjacent to the kitchen. Then I sat down at my computer desk and began to type.

Out of the blue, I envisioned a second big building on the back undeveloped property of Southern Pines. I could easily see a minimum of thirty apartments with beautiful garden windows in each one. A dozen or so freestanding duplexes were arranged in a semi-circle that faced the larger building. In the wee hours of the morning, I designed the entire complex—complete with the charming Mainstreet Mall. *Just one more building project,* I thought with a sigh.

Then I began thinking about Mr. Wade and Mrs. Jessie, who had lived right behind Bo and me in Puzzle

Lake subdivision. They had recently passed away—only a few months apart. Neither one got the chance to live at Southern Pines.

*I know what Mr. Wade would say about me building Phase IV.*

A month later, I met with my partners and shared my latest dream and its spectacular amenities. As always, they were supportive of my newest venture. I was glad we had made the decision two years earlier to purchase another five acres from Mr. Wade. I always thought the day might come when the extra acreage would be needed. My architect, Allen, told me it was adequate land for another *two phases*!

With a new goal in mind, I decided it was necessary to differentiate *Southern Pines Retirement Inn* from *Southern Pines Retirement Community*, the Inn and the Community for short.

*Southern Pines Retirement Community*

"Imagine a town street with sidewalks, small storefronts, Victorian street lamps, and large windows with awnings. There's a restaurant, a barber shop, a gift shop, a post office, and a bank. Now imagine that same street inside the center of a large building. This is the scene—right down to the red and white barber pole and the five-foot-tall black town clock—inside the front entrance of Southern Pines Retirement Community."

*Mainstreet Mall*

I remember how thrilled I was when Allen agreed to meet with me in my office at Southern Pines. I eagerly read the details aloud to him, and he assured me he could envision my biggest dream yet. Week after week, he and I met at his Broad Street office, along with Dennis, the design-builder.

Since Southern Pines was located in my hometown of Thomasville—a quaint and charming town in southwest

Georgia—my intent was to replicate downtown, with its old brick streets, inside of Mainstreet Mall.

In record time, Allen had created architectural drawings for Dennis's construction team. With my imagination and their design expertise, I expected my newest dream to look precisely as I had envisioned—and it did.

Allen located the giant E-shaped brick home directly behind the thirty thousand square-foot front brick building. All thirty-six garden apartments are situated under one single-story roof—with two separate neighborhoods. Each neighborhood features eighteen apartments: eleven one-bedroom, three two-bedroom, and four studio apartments, all with full kitchens. Square footage ranges from 360 to 805 square feet.

Three streets comprise each neighborhood: Tweet Street, Birdie Lane, and Feather Alley make up Birdhouse Village. Church Street, Chapel Drive, and Steeple Court are the streets of Pinecone Village. At the far end of each neighborhood rests a small sitting area named Birdhouse Junction and Pinecone Junction, respectively.

Inside Birdhouse Village one finds the Busy Nest, an appropriate name for a large activity room with a big-screen television and entertainment center.

Wade Chapel, named for my revered and beloved Mr. Wade, is situated in Pinecone Village. When entering the driveway that leads to the Community, the first sight one encounters is the gorgeous stained glass window—a direct reflection of the warm atmosphere of the Southern Pines campus. The cherub wallpaper, along with elegant white church furnishings and deep burgundy carpet, enhance the spiritual atmosphere.

In the midst of the spacious building, where the ceiling

height measures twenty-two feet, is the incredible Mainstreet Mall—with its own downtown!

From my years of experience, I remembered all the places my residents asked to go. My design team and I carefully designed the mall so that residents would not have to leave the campus to shop or dine or bank—unless they just want to.

Inside the mall is Tastee World, a darling little ice cream parlor that resembles a fifties diner, decorated in a Coca Cola theme. The black-and-white checked tile floor adds the perfect finishing touch.

*Tastee World in Mainstreet Mall*

Mainstreet Plaza Restaurant, an elegant dining room, is the location where residents enjoy three delicious home-cooked meals in a family setting. Inside the restaurant one finds a private dining area—the Magnolia Room.

A community library, the Bookshelf, holds a variety

of reading material for residents. A display window in the library and a twelve-foot umbrella tree in the center of the mall are always decorated to reflect the seasons or holidays.

The TLC Clinic is staffed around the clock to meet the residents' emergency needs. The beauty/barber shop, Kut & Kare, provides a full range of beauty care services.

The residents "informed" me that my office would be called Debbie's Place. Debbie's Place stands adjacent to Mainstreet Office, which is affectionately, but appropriately, sometimes referred to as City Hall.

The Mainstreet Message Center, across the street from the Mail Depot, provides residents with a central source for important community information.

Two local banks service the Pine Branch Bank: Check cashing, making deposits, and consultation are services available on-site two mornings each week.

Residents have the opportunity to purchase gifts, cards, and other personal items at the quaint little gift shop, Simply Southern.

Every mall needs public restrooms; ours is no different except that the entrance to the mall restroom sports a purple door adorned with a reflective silver half-moon.

All eight of the storefronts feature different facades: bead board, stucco, brick, board and batten, vertical and horizontal siding, and tin. Each storefront is painted in coordinating bold colors. Six brightly painted benches are randomly placed outside the shops to promote socialization.

Four fifteen-foot-tall black Victorian streetlamps stand sentinel-like in Mainstreet Mall. On either side of the mall, four matching Victorian "city lights" mounted on the wall, nearly twenty feet high, provide an additional warm glow.

A large back porch with a six-foot swing and brown wicker furniture overlooks three spacious courtyards: Rose Arbor, New Beginnings, and Secret Garden. Residents enjoy the gardens. Each garden is planted with lovely flowers, mostly landscape shrubs, day lilies, and crepe myrtles. The sprightly dance of the water from a green concrete fountain accented by a painted brown pinecone on top beckons in the center of the Rose Arbor courtyard. A white picket fence separates the backyard from the remaining undeveloped property.

On the north end of the property behind the apartments stand four charming Victorian cottages in pastel pink, blue, yellow, and green. Plenty of room remains for *Phase V*—twelve additional cottages and a community clubhouse—already developed in my head and on paper.

*Victorian Cottage Community*

With a five thousand square-foot Mall, twenty-nine thousand square feet of living space and corridors in the big building, and two thousand square feet in each duplex, it's no wonder the *Phase IV* expansion is my *multimillion-dollar dream!*

Neither my bankers nor I worried about borrowing another 3.2 million. They knew I could do whatever I set my mind to do and were, in fact, eager to help make the new addition a reality. Although they didn't ask for any cash up front with this huge loan, they did require each partner to sign a personal guaranty.

From an occupancy standpoint, I took a giant risk building the entire complex all at once. Although this time I was fairly certain I wouldn't have booked all forty spaces by opening, I decided this was my final building project, so I wanted to finish it all at the same time. *Famous last words.*

It's a good thing Mama and I started early with the interior furnishings. Because of the size of Mainstreet, there was a lot more to purchase. We needed unusual furnishings, like ice cream parlor equipment, a stamp machine for the post office, and bank furniture.

Selecting the wallpaper and paint colors was a minor concern compared to the bigger decisions—like the top-of-the-line nurse call system and which high-tech security system to order. I rented four metal buildings to store framed prints, kitchenware, and other smaller items while I eagerly waited for construction to end. Meanwhile, I continued to manage the day-to-day operations.

Bo and Mama tried to change my mind about the expansion with words of caution: "Debbie, you really have all the space you need. It'll take more staff to care for the additional residents. "

I always gave the same answer. "Our community needs the additional units to satisfy our aging population, and I'm the most qualified individual to do it."

Although Bo generally let me have the last word, Mama nearly always added her two cents. "You're going to kill yourself trying to keep up. More space will always be needed, but you can't conquer the world."

They heard my heartfelt emotions many times: "At least if I die, you both will know I was happy doing what I enjoy most—taking care of older people. Besides, it's difficult to turn people away due to lack of space."

Approximately six months into the building of *Phase IV*, I was sitting alone in my office at the Inn. Shortly after noon, the residents were making their way to the dining room for lunch when a soft knock on my open door caught me by surprise. I was totally absorbed in preparing the employee work schedule.

As I looked up from my desk, I heard a voice—one that I hardly recognized. For a moment I thought I was dreaming. It couldn't be. Then I recognized her—Mickey's mother.

"Debbie, I couldn't sleep last night. All night I could hear Mickey telling me to come see you—to tell you I'm sorry. I brought his wallet in case you want it. Inside are all the pictures he had of you. I'm really proud of you, Debbie. You have done well, and God has truly blessed you."

As I graciously accepted her apology, we embraced, and I instantly realized my prayer for resolution was finally answered—twenty-three years later! Then I asked if I could add her address to my Southern Pines mailing list. From that day forward, she was aware of the facility's activities listed in our quarterly publication, *Mainstreet Messenger.*

After her departure, I immediately closed my door and went into my tiny bathroom located inside my office. There I stood facing the mirror with tears rolling down my cheeks. At that moment, I envisioned Mickey's smiling face as I quietly whispered a prayer of thanksgiving. After all these years, everything was finally okay.

From a marketing standpoint, I experienced the time of my life sharing my multimillion-dollar concept with the world. It brought new meaning to the words "a small town is like a big family!" In eighteen months, the Community reached full occupancy.

Once the project was complete, individuals came from all over the state to witness the uniqueness of Southern Pines. Most compliments revolved around the interior décor, the immaculate grounds, and the cleanliness and organization inside. Seldom did anyone leave the premises without commenting on the neatly arranged shrubs at the entrance that spelled out the letters: S-P-R-C. It was hard for visitors to believe the entire campus was fully developed in less than four years.

I remember the day of the *Phase IV*/Community Open House. My very first cottage resident moved here from Chicago. She chose her pale blue two-bedroom 1100-square-foot cottage from the architectural drawings. During the festivities, her tears flowed like wine; she was touched when she saw that the end product was even more beautiful and satisfying than she had imagined.

One month after the Community grand opening, I was busy seasonally decorating the umbrella pine tree on Mainstreet when I heard the voice of a former co-worker who had come to see the new addition everyone was talking about … and to apologize for the obscenities she had directed at me that morning in the IV room nearly twelve years earlier. The best part of all was her testimony: "Debbie, I accepted the Lord as my personal Savior. I just wanted you to know."

As I look back, thirty years later, I'm reminded of the minister's words: "The tragedy would not have happened if God had not allowed it, to use it in some way to bless someone."

Perhaps that *someone* he spoke of was my new family—including Bo, Kyle, and me—as well as the hundreds of patients, residents, family members, and employees whose lives have been touched. The experiences I faced during Mickey's life and after his death prepared me well for a purposeful journey.

---

"As long as you're going to think anyway, think big!"
*Donald Trump*

# Chapter 22

## With Dreams Come Heartaches

"All the beautiful sentiments in the world
weigh less than a single lovely action."
*James Russell Lowell*

Along with my multimillion-dollar dream came much heartache. From an outsider's viewpoint, my work looked ever so glamorous. For the most part it was great. However, as both owner *and* executive director, I often walked a precarious line.

When working as director for other facilities, I could easily shift any difficult decisions to the owner who was nowhere around. As *the owner*, I now faced *all* the decisions.

Residents and families had never tried to negotiate rates at my former places of employment, but now those I least expected tried to wheedle a lower rate. *I simply can't negotiate the cost of my utilities or insurance rates,* I reasoned, trying to strengthen my resolve.

Interestingly enough, the adult children who teamed up to pay their parents' fees were far more likely to comply than those adult children who individually had sufficient funds. I never wavered from my company policies; yet, the unrelenting pressure of daily debates with the families exacted a heavy toll. As a compassionate person, I struggle to say no. As a business person, I had to. Holding the line exhausted me.

I recall the lady-friend who notified the State that the staff and I neglected to decorate the facility at Christmas. "If it were said of my facility, then it was spoken without foundation," I told the state inspector. Decorating for *every* holiday was a task I never omitted, even if it meant pulling an all-nighter to get it done.

Unbelievable as it may seem, one resident's middle-aged daughter actually moved in unannounced with her mom. The lady came with file cabinets, books, clothing, and all. She had every intention of staying there while she waited for her new home to be built. The daughter simply couldn't understand my rationale for demanding she relocate.

Then there was the disgruntled son who abruptly moved his prominent father to another facility. When his dad died three days later, he refused to pay either Southern Pines or the other facility.

I still blush a bit each time I remember the napkin incident. A staff member noticed that a resident's son kept taking handfuls of napkins from the dining room for his mother. Once or twice we overlooked it, but this was consistent. Finally, I asked him about it. He had his mother use the napkins as incontinent pads. He refused to purchase Depends for her to use, although money wasn't an issue for the resident.

I couldn't believe my ears the day I heard one son call his mother a b——. Although he was her primary caretaker, as well as her only child, he did not want to deal with the issues at hand. As a direct result of her dementia, his dear, sweet mom had started wandering aimlessly from apartment to apartment. "I am not moving her to another facility," he said resolutely. It didn't matter to him that she was infringing on the rights of other residents. Or that she was now in an unsafe environment. I had to call upon my attorneys to deal with that troubling situation.

Southern Pines provides "catered care," which is our term for additional personal care services that residents need as their health and mental abilities decline. In spite of the fact that families often witnessed or even experienced personally a parent's need for additional personal care services, many balked at the idea of paying for it.

In one circumstance an issue arose that I was never totally able to resolve. A sweet little resident accumulated stuff and never discarded anything. Eventually, she had only a narrow path through her cram-packed room. Every week I had to confront her and remind her that her room was a safety and fire hazard not only to herself, but to the entire facility. In truth, I worked among a ton of packrats in my twenty-year tenure. Folks simply couldn't understand what the problem was when their space became not only a safety hazard but a fire hazard that could not be allowed to continue. All they saw were prized memories and personal belongings.

Although I employed qualified on-call staff, seldom did an entire weekend go by that either Bo or I (or both) didn't get called for something: mostly "owner-type" issues that involved the actual building or major equipment. One Saturday night phone call in particular stands out. Against company policy, a family member had, for more than an hour, blocked the drive-thru at the Inn. A visitor who could wait no longer attempted to drive around the obtrusive car. In so doing, the person knocked the water faucet completely off the outside of the building. Five hours later, midnight, Bo and I were still with the plumber. The following week I received a bill for several hundred dollars. That was the only mishap for which the individual involved voluntarily offered to pay for the damage.

The most heart-wrenching episode occurred when two out-of-town daughters blamed the management team for their mother's death after their mother was transferred from the Community to the Inn to get the care she so desperately needed. The girls just couldn't imagine their mother leaving her 540-square-feet apartment to live in a 312-square-feet suite. So often, family reaction wasn't about proper care of the resident. It was more about space and prestige. My staff and I could clearly see it was strictly what the adult children wanted rather than what was in Mom's or Dad's best interest. Unfortunately, this kind of incident was not an occasional occurrence. Truthfully, these tense and often argumentative family conferences caused me to want to throw in the towel.

My employees were another story altogether. Although I referred to most of my employees as "saints," some were not always so saintly. I did face my fair share of problems, exactly the way other employers do.

Personnel problems didn't disappear even when I was engulfed in personal grief. The night my daddy died, a formerly reliable caregiver abruptly decided she didn't want to work nights with her co-worker anymore. Instead of finishing her night shift, she walked off the job at 1:30

a.m. without even letting the on-call supervisor know. She just walked out. Right then. Right there. In the middle of the night! The co-worker on duty decided to work the rest of the night alone, even though working alone violated company policy. The administrator assuming weekend call duty alerted me to the situation. All the employees knew company policy did not permit working shorthanded, especially during the night when anything could happen and support staff or administrators could not be called upon for help. The next week the disgruntled employee and I discussed her actions. She just couldn't understand why she should not be allowed to return to work when it suited her. Through the entire ordeal, I kept thinking, *I'm not even allowed time to deal with my own grief.*

Another gut-wrenching facet of my work was dealing with residents with regard to employees. The residents become extremely dependent on their caregivers and want to be attended by their favorite staff member—no matter what. Anytime I had to discharge an employee, the residents expected me to share with them the details. Explanations about labor regulations, company policies, and procedures or confidentiality issues never sufficed. They simply knew that their caregiver was gone.

On a Friday morning, shortly before lunch, my insurance agent came to review the annual liability insurance policy, which was up for renewal in three days. That conversation and review triggered a major business dilemma. I always expected a modest annual increase in business expenses and especially with insurance premiums. However, I was appalled when the agent informed me the rate had increased from $35,000 to $147,000, a staggering 420% increase. He described it as an industry-wide price hike. As a one-facility owner, I didn't have the option of spreading the cost over several buildings. That incident became one of the fourteen reasons why I knew the time was right to sell Southern Pines.

Now that I had the massive liability premium staring me in the face, I agonized for weeks over cutting back employees. Although it was a prudent financial and business decision, I ached when I had to reduce staff. That ache intensified when the effected staff refused to see my side of the issue.

In the early stages of development of *Phase IV*, I had convinced myself that the operation side of my multimillion-dollar dream would be a breeze. After all, I had done it before with great success. I reasoned that incoming residents would be able to meet their own personal needs, that they had just grown tired of maintaining a home and yard. Besides, I was content knowing I didn't have to follow the yellow book of guidelines since the Community was not classified as an assisted living facility.

It didn't take long to realize how I had underestimated the challenges. Within two years after the Community opened, twenty-five percent of the first independent residents "aged in place," and, in time, needed additional long-term care. At Southern Pines that always mandated a move from the Community to the Inn. With nearly every move, the resident or family member resented the decision-maker in the assessment, whether it was me or one of my administrators.

Occasionally, we faced another huge dilemma: either the facility was full at the Inn or the resident's needs violated the state regulations. That ultimately meant nursing home placement was essential. Families always blamed me or the staff for the inability to meet the resident's needs at his or her current level of contract. They simply did not want to hear about state regulations. Neither did they want to confront the reality of an aging, failing parent. It wasn't long before I came to *dread* family conferences involving the move of a resident.

Within three years of the Community's opening, nearly fifty percent of the independent residents needed assisted living care. After careful consideration, my partners and I agreed to spend another fifty thousand dollars to add a fire wall—a thick, one hour fire-resistant wall built in the attic directly above Mainstreet Mall—to prevent the spread of fire between the mall and the two adjoining neighborhoods. That improvement was required by the state fire marshal before the State Health Planning Agency would issue a certificate of need. Attaining a certificate of need was in itself a seemingly endless, frustrating, and costly process that felt like a full-time job. For me, it was as huge as writing a business plan all over again. Finally, the Community was granted a license, and it was no longer necessary for the residents to relocate to the Inn. However, we faced a new quandary. To cover the cost of the fire wall, I had no choice but to raise the rates. Residents couldn't understand why the rates were higher at the Community than the Inn. They didn't take into consideration that the Community apartments were nearly double the size of the Inn suites. The truth of the matter was, it proved to be a no-win situation either way.

Within six years of Southern Pines' original opening, at least thirty percent of the residents at the Inn required dementia care. Converting nineteen assisted living spaces at the Inn to dementia care suites meant the installation of door codes to secure the unit, along with a significant increase in staff training. There was never a time that my staff and I didn't go overboard trying our best to meet the needs of our aging population. Surprisingly, just eighteen months after the creation of the dementia unit took place, I informed the maintenance staff that we needed to revert the unit to regular assisted living again. The insurance premiums mandated that draining move. Providing for residents who may become violent, climb out the windows, or wander off, in spite of our best efforts, was a liability that I later realized my company could not endure. Although we made every effort to accommodate the changing needs of our residents, it seemed that by the time we became accustomed to doing things one way, it was time to change again. Caring for the aged is very difficult to plan. No one can predict length of life or the rate at which personal capabilities will decline.

As the campus grew, so did the stressful situations that daily dropped in my lap as the owner. Because of the expansions, the campus required additional management staff. I could no longer handle the administrative and management duties alone, so I created two administrator positions—one for the Inn and one for the Community—and hired exceedingly qualified individuals. Two well-trained key employees decided they didn't want to answer to anyone but me, so they left.

These were just a few of the many episodes that gave me the shove I needed to sell. For the sake of my health, the time finally came for me to separate myself from Southern Pines.

With both Mama and Bo on site, there was seldom a moment when the topic of discussion didn't revolve around Southern Pines. In truth, we had no life apart from the business. At night I listened to Bo vent about those who violated the signs and policies and encroached on his neatly manicured lawns or blocked the drive-thru so the ambulance couldn't get to the entrance. Bo fumed when guests parked in the clearly marked parking spaces reserved only for residents because he then had to tell the visitors to move their vehicles. Such incidents required constant, unpleasant, and unnecessary confrontations. My heart broke knowing Bo worked so hard and was as overwhelmed as I with things we could not control.

Although Mama meant well, she always told me every little bitty thing that happened at the Inn. Serving as a Pine Pal and volunteering her time meant the world to me, but, like Bo, she didn't realize the emotional energy it took for me to deal with nonstop issues.

On the other hand, Bo and Mama were my sounding board. They willingly listened to me and my grievances. It was no doubt harder for them than for me, as they watched my health deteriorate before their very eyes.

As the campus grew, so did the business income, along with the tax liability. Tax matters were unquestionably the most challenging issues I had ever faced. My passion for the hands-on work with seniors led me to neglect that part of the business from the outset. I had simply assumed I'd be paying the usual one-third of my salary in taxes. Though I was an owner in a limited liability company, being a working partner resulted in an even greater tax burden. Little did I know that my tax obligations would reach an all-time high of nearly fifty percent of my total earnings! My accountant worked diligently to seek creative, yet honest and legal ways to help me overcome the enormous taxes I owed.

Although I built Southern Pines from the heart, at times I did find myself asking my accountant a very heartfelt and sensible business question: "Why am I working twice as hard in my own business to keep only half as much as if I were an employee?"

I paid forty-nine percent of the profits to my partners first. Then out of my share of the profits, I paid almost one-half for federal and state taxes. I felt as if I were in a no-win situation, especially when I worked both night and day.

Looking back, I have no regrets regarding my choice to build my own business. But the stress of the daily grind of a business that never closed and the tax ramifications are matters most entrepreneurs do not take into consideration. For their own sake, they really should.

Entrepreneurship does have amazing advantages, but also its great disadvantages creep in constantly. I learned the hard way *from experience.* Should I choose to become an entrepreneur again, without a doubt I'll be far more knowledgeable, and I'll have a much better handle on what to expect. No one will ever have to convince me that being bigger is not always better!

---

"When we are no longer able to change a situation … we are challenged to change ourselves."
*Viktor Frankl*

# Chapter 23

## Above and Beyond ... the Call

"The true measure of success lies not so much in what you have achieved, but in knowing that you have touched the lives of others."
*Anonymous*

"Are you *really* taking residents on a Caribbean cruise to the Bahamas?" Sheila, Miss Ruth's granddaughter, asked. "Remember, my grandmother is one hundred years old!"

"Yep, I am. We're leaving the Sunday after Thanksgiving," I answered. "And I'm not too worried about Miss Ruth as agile as she is."

"Wow, Debbie ... All I can say is you're braver than I am," Sheila remarked.

"Aren't you afraid to take a chance with that many old folks?" Miss Smith's son questioned. "What if they get sick while you're gone?"

"Not worried the least bit. We'll have a big time. If they get sick, well, remember I'm a nurse. Besides, there is a medical staff onboard," I replied confidently.

It didn't matter to me that the staff and I had loads of paperwork to complete, including a medical file for each one taking the trip. I knew advance medications had to be ordered. I understood the numerous liabilities involved. Regardless, I intended to do everything possible to add to my residents' quality of life and their precious memories.

A year after completing my multimillion-dollar dream, seven residents, the activities director, and I loaded onto a chartered bus. From Cape Canaveral we were off to Nassau and Coco Cay for a four-day excursion.

Not only was Miss Ruth my oldest resident at Southern Pines, but she was also the eldest guest to ever sail on a Royal Caribbean cruise ship. Because Miss Ruth was a centenarian, we all enjoyed additional fringe benefits, such as a personal visit with the captain, a tour of his quarters, and a memorable one hundredth birthday party honoring Miss Ruth the final night.

Two years later, Bo joined me to chaperone another group of residents on a seven-day cruise. Our destination—the Cayman Islands via the cruise liner Imagination. This time the group numbered eighteen, including some family members who also signed up. However, without Bo there was no way I'd have been bold enough to tackle that large number of attendees. Truthfully, we each felt more secure knowing that he was coming too.

Not a day went by that the ladies didn't love having Bo near. They knew he could fix just about anything at Southern Pines. More than that, they loved his caring ways and teasing personality, especially when he'd slip up behind them and tickle their necks. Whether it was morning, noon, or middle of the afternoon, when that tickle occurred, without the slightest look behind them, they always knew it was Bo. He loved the Southern Pines family as much as I did.

At the Rock-A-Thon each February, we raised money for the American Heart Association. Chairs were lined across the front porch. For two hours residents would rock nonstop while entertainment took place. Perhaps a clown would visit, or we might have special music or a hula-hoop contest. Sponsors supported the residents who rocked the entire time.

At the annual Valentine's Banquet there was always the selection of a King and Queen and a lovely sweetheart dinner with individual heart cakes displayed on each table. Door prizes, gift exchanges, fresh flowers, balloons, and sweetheart music were the order of the evening. Residents could hardly wait to see what gifts Bo and I exchanged—the banquet at Southern Pines always took the place of our *own* sweetheart outing.

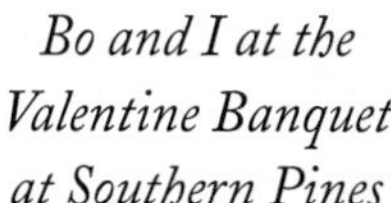

*Bo and I at the Valentine Banquet at Southern Pines*

During May, special events celebrate "Older Americans Month" all over the country. At Southern Pines, the celebration often took the form of a country and western night with cloggers, square dancers, and an outdoor cookout. Bo would grill hamburgers and hot-dogs. As always, in his shadow was Kyle, now a teenager, who the residents claimed as their collective grandson.

When home from military school, Kyle's presence was coveted by his numerous grandparents. During Happy Hour they opted to hear his stories of life at Riverside Military Academy. From the eighth grade through his senior year, Kyle spent his school days in Gainesville, Georgia, but he always devoted his summers to working at Southern Pines.

*Our son, Kyle, graduates from Riverside Military Academy, 2002*

On the display board located in the dining room, the night staff listed the activities for the next day. I especially remember the morning we all read the board: only twelve days left before Kyle would be home! Mr. Lawson told me nearly every week: "I wrote Kyle a letter today." He suggested Southern Pines host a "coming-home" party for him. And that we did.

It often touched my heart when Mr. Lawson's sister, Miss Emily, prayed for our young cadet every time she asked the noonday blessing. It was obvious they all loved Kyle. No wonder Miss Anna always asked me if he could be the *one* to transport her to the doctor.

Rose, the night supervisor, routinely asked me to let him work anytime there was a call-in on her shift. "Just send me Kyle," she begged, especially during those times when there was little notice of an employee's absence.

June is Bride's Month in the outside world, and with our bi-annual mock wedding, June was bridal month for us too. Each year one chosen couple eagerly agreed to serve as bride and groom. Yes, the "older" bride always donned a gorgeous wedding gown, while the groom, often in his mid-nineties, dressed in a black tuxedo. The preacher was there along with traditional wedding music, bridesmaids, ushers, and flower girls. A wedding reception complete with cake and punch followed the ceremony. The simulated celebration honored the cumulative years of marriage represented by the entire Southern Pines family: One year the total was 2,696 years; another year, 3,742. No doubt, the bi-annual June wedding was the most cherished and sentimental event of all celebrations.

"Debbie, will you please sign me up for Computer 101?" my ninety-nine-year-old resident asked. "It will take place at Southern Pines, won't it?"

"Ms. Mac, I'll be happy to reserve a space for you. Yes, ma'am, it's happening every Tuesday in the Robin's Nest at the Inn. The computer is in place and ready to go. I'm naming this group the Senior Surfers."

On the Fourth of July, we all anticipated Bo's famous barbequed Boston butts—grilled to perfection, using his dad's recipe. Even if it meant cooking all night, we knew it would be ready by noon.

Bo's favorite little resident, Mr. Glynn, at the age of ninety-something, always covered for Bo so he could take breaks. "Now, Debbie, you make sure Bo gets plenty of rest," he reminded me. "Don't let him work too hard. After all, you know he's been up all night cooking for us." Mr. Glynn loved Bo and was excited the day Bo gave him a pair of navy suspenders. Just like me, my husband was always giving to the residents. Providing for the folks so dear to us was an awesome experience.

Each September, the governor proclaimed "Assisted Living Week in Georgia" to recognize the importance of care facilities in the lives of seniors. Each year, I also recruited our mayor, who would declare Wednesday of that special week as "Assisted Living Day in Thomasville." We made the day memorable by picnicking at the lake, watching the Dancing Raisinettes, and listening to the local college jazz band.

Just as my local town hosted an annual "Victorian Christmas," so did Southern Pines. I dressed in my full length, custom made plaid Victorian skirt, and Bo donned his black slacks, matching vest, and black beanie cap. I remember the year nearly 350 guests attended the gala. Bo helped the residents and visitors on and off the carriage rides when he wasn't parking cars or moving extension cords around for the musicians. Meanwhile, residents browsed the shops and the staff served holiday goodies.

Mainstreet Mall was the perfect location for the community-wide gala: carriage rides, old-fashioned tea cakes, hot chocolate, apple cider, Santa Claus, and freeze models. Musicians provided lovely holiday music inside Mainstreet and under the portico. Volunteers provided gift wrapping in Simply Southern. A kids' shopping corner bustled with activity in Busy Nest. A Mennonite bake sale was in full swing at Tastee World. Storytelling: The real reason for the season was shared in Wade Chapel. It was always the *biggest* event of the year!

*Bo at Victorian Gala with freeze models at Southern Pines*

Every year on the eve of Christmas Eve, residents were instructed to leave a shoe outside their door. Shortly after midnight, Mama and I would quietly roam the streets of Southern Pines and slip a special little gift in each shoe. I'm not sure who was the most excited, the residents or me! The next morning they eagerly brought their surprises to share during breakfast.

Monthly tea parties featured different themes like a Beanie Baby tea, *Chicken Soup for the Soul* tea, Mother's and Father's Day teas, as well as Thanksgiving, St. Patrick's, and an Easter Sunday tea.

The residents participated in the monthly town hall meetings. One resident assumed the role of mayor—just like at a real city council meeting. At these meetings residents joined in planning special events like Police 101, book reviews, musical programs, special speakers, and the biggest decision of all—the location of their next monthly dinner outing.

Each New Year's Eve, shortly before midnight, the Southern Pines family gathered in Wade Chapel for a special communion service led by Reverend Hugh Rockett and his sweet wife, Bonnie. It was our way of bringing in the New Year together as a family. Fellowship always followed in Mainstreet with popcorn and Coke.

But my favorite part of the dream was the *time* I spent with my Southern Pines residents—listening intently as they eagerly shared years of history and wisdom with me.

I equally honored and recognized my loyal staff. For the most part they made my job much easier. Since company policy didn't allow for gratuities from the residents, I established the "Fun Jar" idea. Any tips were accumulated in Mainstreet Office throughout the year. Then, the first of December, each resident was encouraged to contribute twenty dollars in lieu of buying individual employee gifts. All Fun Jar proceeds were evenly distributed among a loving and faithful staff—those with a minimum six-month tenure. I remember one Christmas when fifty-eight employees received ninety dollars each, which confirmed my belief that the staff had made a tremendous difference in the lives of our residents.

There was a constant struggle to convince the residents to honor the "no tip" policy. They all wanted to show their gratitude toward their special caregivers. They simply didn't understand the problems caused by the violation of this policy; it was easy for employees to get their feelings hurt.

Then there was the "Caught You Caring" program, where residents and families contributed their accolades in writing on a card. Each quarter the employee with the highest number of caring comments was recognized. The winner received several rewards: a reserved parking space for three months, one hundred dollars cash, a restaurant gift certificate, a plaque, and a celebration with a cake in his or her honor.

The employees enjoyed the annual "let down" at the Employee Christmas Party—usually held off campus. Sometimes it took place at Mr. Groover's Sugar Mill Clubhouse. Other times I booked the Vashti Conference Center. Most years Bo, Kyle, and I invited them to drop by our home for a time of food, fun, and fellowship and a surprise Christmas gift.

I'll never forget the year the maintenance guys, Bo and Sonny, entertained us all with their rendition of the song "Take This Job and Shove It." Their rendition really brought the house down. Laughter prevailed and we were all in stitches with tears streaming down our cheeks. Without Bo and Kyle to pitch in, there is no way I could have gone *above and beyond the call of duty*. They were indispensable to the incredible success of my wonderful Southern Pines.

---

"Most people never run far enough on their
first wind to find out if they've got a second.
Give your dreams all you've got, and you'll be
amazed at the energy that comes out of you."
*William James*

# Chapter 24

## Work, Work, Work

"I was pushed back and about to fall,
but the Lord helped me."
*Psalm 118:13*

So much of who I am is where I have been.

*I'm in a hurry to get things done. I rush and rush until life's no fun. All I have to do is live and die, but I'm in a hurry and don't know why.* Those lyrics from a song by Alabama described my life to a T.

*If I die tomorrow, it'll be okay. I'm doing what I love, what God called me to do,* I told myself hundreds of times. But the truth was, weekends and holidays always placed a damper on my mood. Nothing took the place of work!

"Have you prepared for an early death?" The question hit me like a ton of bricks! I didn't have a clue what she was trying to tell me. Her warning continued: "Unless you are ready to die, you'd better make important lifestyle changes now!"

For the past two decades, my home life and my work life were indistinct from one another, as inseparable as my shadow. Many witnessed firsthand the toll those endless all-nighters had on my well-being, while others could see I had finally reached my limit.

For me, a typical day often started in the middle of the night. Assuming that I even went to bed, that is. This particular morning I crawled out of my warm cozy bed at three a.m.

*If Bo awakens, he'll know where I am.*

I tugged on my old favorite navy sweatpants and striped shirt and off I trailed to Debbie's Place. I needed to get Mr. Johnson's admission chart put together. With all the interruptions that had occurred yesterday, I didn't finish decorating the umbrella pine in Mainstreet Mall. The resident council meeting was scheduled for eleven a.m., and I had yet to prepare my notes. Moreover, I needed to complete the employee evaluation for one of the night shift staff.

*After getting all these business issues out of the way, I'll be well prepared for the day.*

At 5:50 a.m., I finished my preliminary duties. Grabbing my shopping list, I hopped in the company van. As soon as I turned the corner at the Hardees drive-thru window and said "Good morning," the nice lady had my order ready: a sausage biscuit with four mustards and a medium Diet Coke—my fix for twenty years. I was nearly always her first customer at six a.m. sharp.

Sitting in the Wal-Mart parking lot, I wolfed down my breakfast, hardly tasting it, and then rushed inside to hurriedly purchase all the items on my list. I was on the road again and returned home to dress for my "real" workday. By eight o'clock, I was decked out in my usual business casual and making my way through the dining room of each facility with a cheerful "Good morning."

Since I had come to work at 3:10 a.m., I felt sure I could finish my day by five o'clock p.m. Before Bo got home from work that evening, I planned to run by Mama's house to visit for a few minutes.

Just as I was ready to leave for the day, a frail silver-haired lady and her handsome son entered the mall.

"We're looking for the little lady who owns this place."

His mother was contemplating a move to Southern Pines, and they wanted to take a look at the campus as well as discuss the stipulations of her long-term care insurance policy. My physician friend recommended they talk directly with me. I knew I couldn't leave. Besides, no one could market my business the way I could.

At seven p.m., Bo picked me up at the mall entrance, and we quickly headed to Burger King to grab a bite to eat before he dropped me back off at Debbie's Place. I needed to complete a couple of things I had forgotten. "If I can get the stack of papers off my desk, it'll make me sleep better tonight," I told him. Bo had heard that story many times; nonetheless, he always understood. He was sound asleep when I tiptoed in at two a.m.

Another close friend, Billie Jo, a physical therapy assistant, stopped by my office every morning as she made rounds. She worked with the company who handled most of our residents' rehabilitation needs.

I recall the morning Russ told her I was at home sick, a rarity for me. She knew it was the day of the annual formal tea party, a fundraising event for our own Southern Charm Garden Club. Billie Jo knew immediately something was seriously wrong. I never missed events.

Billie Jo quickly made her way to our home in Puzzle Lake, coming through the garage and inside the back door to the master bedroom. There I lay in my queen-size bed with my head buried in my big, soft feather pillow. I seldom experienced headaches, but this one was relentless. For hours I had been vomiting and couldn't get out of bed. Later the diagnosis was confirmed: stress and lack of sleep.

Shortly thereafter, I decided to give my friend Sandra, a geriatric psychologist, a call. We talked often regarding my residents, so I knew she was a good listener.

"Now what's so wrong with me taking such good care of my folks?" I asked. She knew I was now working over one hundred hours a week, but then she told me truthfully and directly what I didn't want to hear!

"Debbie, you are an adrenaline junkie! It's the adrenaline fix that is allowing you to stay up night after night without the rest your body needs," she explained. "You're going to have a heart attack and die! You've got to make a change—now," she challenged me.

She already knew I employed administrators and managers to manage the day-to-day duties of the business. She was also aware that we had bought Bantam Bend, our mountain home, as a means of escape. Sandra knew we had purchased our gorgeous royal blue 1800 Honda Gold Wing trike—Bo's long-awaited retirement toy—intending to get away from the stresses of the business.

*Bo and I on our 1800 Honda Gold Wing Trike*

She heard me say more than once that Bo and I lived in a "glass house." She remembered last Thanksgiving when I told her a family member had come to our personal residence shortly after lunch to report, "Mama's hair didn't get combed today."

That incident was the first time I could recall Bo *really* losing his temper. "We should be allowed a holiday in peace in our own home," he said angrily with a sense of disappointment in his voice. I couldn't have agreed more. Living across the street from the facility proved to be too much for us both during our last two years in the business.

As maintenance supervisor, Bo and I had recruited two wonderful and talented maintenance guys to manage in his absence. So, he was finally able to distance himself a little, except for the on-call duties, the last couple of years of our ownership.

For me, however, it was different. Though the families

didn't purposely seek to wear me out, they didn't want to deal with anyone but me. In their minds, it didn't matter that I employed qualified management staff. It was simple: For them, Southern Pines was a paid employee and they chose not to stop till they got to the top!

I had no awareness until my last year at Southern Pines as I chatted with Sandra that I was dealing with an actual disorder called *work addiction*. Only after her stern warning did I feel compelled to pay attention to what my body had been trying to tell me. *Whatever has a hold on me, I have to let it go.*

She told me there is always an underlying reason why an individual works endlessly. She said it even happens in ministry. Although I didn't know the answer to my dilemma, I was determined to find it.

The scariest part for me was when she told me that the final symptom of work addiction is spiritual bankruptcy. "It heralds a dead end," she said. I already knew I had no choice but to change. I couldn't make good decisions anymore. But I was so frightened. I was scared out of my wits. I knew the time had come. The time was here, now. *I had to make that big decision!* I finally realized that I could not help others if I didn't help myself first!

---

"Don't hurry, don't worry. You're only here for a short visit. So be sure to stop and smell the roses."
*Walter Hagen*

# Chapter 25
## Making the Big Decision

"If we trust our intuition and respond, it's always right, because we're open enough to see what to do."
*Paul Horn*

*How do I go about making the big decision? How can I really know, beyond the shadow of a doubt, that the time is right to let go of my big dream?* Though my head told me one thing, my heart told me something altogether different. *If only Bo or someone would just tell me what to do…*

Over the past few months each time Bo and I frequented the Tallahassee Mall, I made a beeline to the "business" section of Barnes and Noble while he stood in line to purchase our favorite chocolate-chip Frappuccino. As I searched high and low for just the right book, the perfect book—the one that would tell me exactly when to sell my business, I was certain there was such a book out there. Somewhere! *Surely there are other business owners experiencing the same issues*, I told myself. My emotions were so frazzled that I simply didn't trust my own intuition. I was not successful in locating "that book."

"Deb, I honestly wish I knew what to tell you," Bo commented more than once during our conversations regarding the big decision. One Sunday morning, as he sat in his oak rocker, his feet propped on the gliding ottoman in the living room of our Puzzle Lake home, he began to share openly: "I know how much you love the residents and staff. I understand what you are going through, Deb. I want you to be happy." Then, after a brief pause, he added, "I want you to be healthy. I don't want to bury a young wife. I want us to grow old together. But I'll support you in whatever decision you make."

"Mom, it's your decision," Kyle commented. "Dad and I just want what's best for you and for Southern Pines. We know how hard you've worked. And we understand the emotional dilemma. But we can't make the decision for you."

---

Another one of my all-night flings was unfolding! Yet this one felt different. Now my mind was made up! At least that's how I felt after working the night shift (as well as the day shift) for the umpteenth time since I had expanded my business. Nine years ago I built Southern Pines Retirement Community. Completing four phases of development in three years and eight months that culminated in a campus covering 8.1 acres had worn me to a frazzle. As the number of employees increased from eleven to nearly seventy, I constantly wrestled with the challenge of finding good, reliable employees. Because I wanted only the best for my facility as well as for the people who called Southern Pines home, I often worked those vacant positions as I diligently sought to find honest, reputable, and compassionate employees. This was in addition to my responsibilities as executive director and owner.

On this particular night, amidst all the other duties I had to get done before my normal workday began, I set aside my busy work. I felt compelled to write a letter to each of my business partners. In the letter, I detailed fourteen reasons why now was the time to sell Southern Pines. None of the points mentioned that my body was worn out, that I could not continue this pace. I never wanted even the slightest whim of that thought to enter the picture. It *had* to be the right time for the business sale, not necessarily the right time for me.

Looking out for everyone else's best interests always took precedence over meeting my own needs. That's the way I had lived my whole life. To admit to exhaustion meant to admit to defeat! I believed I was supposed to keep on going no matter what.

I hid that letter in my locked desk drawer for one solid week. I needed time to ponder my decision. I wanted to be absolutely certain of my choice. A few months before I had considered selling, even to the point of bringing up the subject with my accountant and a couple of my attorney partners. But in no time flat, I changed my mind. Just the mere thought of leaving behind my dream facility—two large buildings and four Victorian cottages—seemed way more than I could fathom. Not to mention the anxiety I felt as I contemplated leaving the residents whom I cared so deeply about. They had become my second family (and sometimes it seemed even my first family). Because my heart and soul permeated every inch of Southern Pines, I knew that letting go would be difficult at best.

The thought of selling would surface periodically, especially when I'd become overly tired or on those days when, despite the best efforts of the staff or myself, we apparently could not satisfy family members. Residents and staff were always easier to deal with than family members. Family members usually made life pleasant for those of us who worked to take care of their loved ones. But there were those moments that sometimes seemed like hours, occasionally like days, in which those wonderful family members could drive us to want to pull out our hair. We could never escape the high expectations or unreasonable demands of some families.

After twenty-five years of service, Bo had retired from the United Parcel Service three years earlier in order to assist me. Without even a day of rest between jobs, he assumed full-time responsibility as maintenance supervisor—a job he felt comfortable doing considering he had spent nearly every evening as well as every Saturday working at Southern Pines several years prior to his early retirement.

This night fling emerged in the wee hours of the morning. Nestled in my comfy forest green office chair, I began writing my letter. For me to write to the individuals who had supported me in my endeavor meant I was serious. Truly this was not just an emotional, off-the-wall feeling. It was a bit frightening, even for me.

Making the personal decision to sell Southern Pines Retirement Community was the most heart-wrenching decision of my life. Nonetheless, I knew I had to do it. Just as sure as I knew my name, I knew I had to do it—for myself primarily, but also for my partners. In order to maintain the level of care that I wanted for the residents, I just *had* to do it.

One week after my late night letter-writing escapade, I surprised a number of businessmen when I appeared at their individual businesses to announce to them, in writing, my decision to sell Southern Pines. As I met with each of these business partners, I encouraged them to make their own decision as to whether or not they wanted to remain an owner in the business. It was the right and fair option since it honored the specifics of our operating agreement.

Not one of the partners, in spite of the unprecedented success of the company and the high-paying quarterly dividends, wanted to remain in the business without my presence as executive director. The partners could easily have purchased my fifty-one percent stock in the company. They could have continued getting the dividend checks. But the thought of hiring a competent director, who genuinely *cared* about the business, was an arduous task they elected not to face. From a distance my partners had watched my ongoing futile efforts (especially since the fourth expansion) to find that right person to fill my shoes as executive director. They knew my intention was to get some relief so that I could continue as owner for years to come. When I came calling with my letter, they were ready to get out right along with me.

During the time I was recruiting a buyer, one of my eleven partners literally begged me to reconsider the big decision to sell. He was not only concerned about the loss of business income, but he was also worried. "Debbie, how will you stop work so abruptly? I just can't see you letting Southern Pines go, not just like that. You really need to think about your decision." He knew I had set up the business loan so that it would be paid in full by the time I reached age fifty-five, but the truth of the matter was, I simply couldn't make it. The endless hours of overworking had taken its toll. So for me, there was absolutely no turning back… No talking me out of it!

To my amazement and relief, the very day I delivered the news of my decision every partner willingly signed the document, confirming, "If you are selling, so am I!"

With my decision made and endorsed by the partners, I knew I had work to do. I speculated that finding a buyer for an amazingly successful company like Southern Pines wouldn't take long. I just knew there was someone out there who'd be interested in purchasing my show facility, but it was more than scouting for "just a buyer." I had to find the *right* buyer. The buyer had to be committed to continuing my mission of providing quality care for my special residents. I could do no less for those I had come to love.

A simple phone call to my liability insurance underwriter during the time I was shopping rates identified one potential buyer within a few weeks. A couple of additional e-mails landed two more interested prospects. Each asked what seemed like a million questions. They not only wanted to visit the facility, but they also requested a ton of information *prior* to their visit: financial statements, census history reports, architectural plans, land surveys, lists of residents and employees, payroll reports, and other legal paperwork. That meant confidentiality contracts had to be established. At first it didn't seem so awesome until I began triplicating all the documents. All of this was in addition to handling my "beyond full" daily schedule.

From that day forward, my emotions took me on a rollercoaster ride. Being so overly drained didn't help matters in the least. As any responsible owner would do for the sake of the business as well as the residents' and staff's security, I kept the plan to myself. Except for my partners and my immediate family, truly no one else knew for months.

One of my partners, an attorney, took time to visit with me regularly at the facility. I cherished our conversations because I could speak openly with him. He provided his legal insight. He recognized that the undertaking would be emotionally draining for me. I had built Southern Pines from my heart.

I had no idea how long it might take to complete the process, down to the handing over of the keys to a new owner. I had no inkling of how marketable such a business was. What I did know was that I didn't want to use a brokerage company. I would have to gather all the information for a broker anyway, so I figured I might as well handle the entire process myself. My attorney partner suggested it would take at least a year.

I wondered if I had waited a bit too long to start the process. For me, a year seemed like forever. I was past the point of exhaustion. Even with my workaholic tendencies, I could finally see that it was simply not possible for any one human being to carry such an enormous load for the long haul. Then my workaholic mindset kicked in and I knew I would bring the project to completion, just as I had everything else I had ever started.

Six months into the "For Sale" project, I desperately needed some additional help with the handling of extra paperwork. I turned to Russ, my talented office manager. Four years earlier, Russ had been a godsend when I hired him as my administrative assistant. Russ was as articulate, trustworthy, and dependable as I had hoped he would be. Russ was the only male I had ever hired to work with me in the office. He became the perfect administrative assistant. Russ never divulged any of Southern Pines' business. He patiently and caringly attended to the residents when they showed up at his office window. He quietly covered for me when he recognized that my energy was depleted. Russ bailed me out many times as we waited for the right buyer. No wonder I recruited him as my greatest confidant as the days and months slowly passed.

My partners had always been silent in the operations of the business, so for them the business sale was merely a wait-and-see proposition. For me, life had become a circus. Keeping the business operating at optimum, while secretly entertaining three potential buyers without showing signs of complete exhaustion, became an emotional nightmare.

I had always declared to whomever asked that I was committed to remain the owner and director of Southern Pines as long as my health allowed. I was determined to keep the business long enough to pay off the debt completely. Only seven years of payments remained. For a long time, I prayed for strength to honor the commitment I had made to myself and expressed to others. I never imagined that I would actively seek to sell my business while I was still forty-something.

Deep within, I knew, I absolutely knew that I had made a significant difference in the lives of the many residents and staff members during the twenty-plus years in which I had built and developed Southern Pines in my hometown. I also knew I had become physically, emotionally, and spiritually bankrupt.

I readily accepted the fact that the people who cared about me would understand. Those that didn't understand had never walked in my shoes. The bottom line was the time had come... *Southern Pines had to be sold.*

---

"Everything that has a beginning has an ending.
Make your peace with that and all will be well."
*Anonymous*

# Chapter 26

## The Longest Year

"The greatest use of life is to spend it
for something that will outlast it."
*William James*

The fifteen-month span it took to sell Southern Pines was strenuous in itself without added complications. Exactly four weeks from the day I delivered the news to my partners, I faced another exhausting chain of events.

My mama had just retired after twenty-three years of employment as manager of the record shop. She then came to work at Southern Pines as a Pine Pal, a private sitter hired by a resident.

Anytime Mama was scheduled to work, she always arrived early to visit with Peggy, the beauty operator. When Mama didn't show up at the salon Monday morning, Peggy became concerned. Since Bo and I were out of town, Peggy asked Carolyn, a mutual friend, to drive to Mama's house, only four blocks away, to check on her.

One hour later, Mama was transported by ambulance to

the emergency room. Peggy called me in North Carolina. Mama had been admitted to the hospital.

Three years earlier, Bo and I had purchased a charming three-story log home in the mountains of North Carolina. We had high hopes of taking desperately needed time away in the peaceful countryside. But every time we tried to go, something major occurred at Southern Pines. Our mini-vacations were often terminated prematurely before we ever had a chance to unwind. Although the circumstances were different this time, the results were the same. Bo and I hurriedly packed our bags to return home.

As we traveled the Interstate, my cell phone rang. It was Mama's doctor. "Debbie, your mother has suffered a cerebral vascular accident with left-sided involvement," he explained. "Her condition is stable." Unfortunately, by the time Bo and I got home six hours later, Mama had suffered a second stroke. This one was much more debilitating than the first.

My experience as a gerontology nurse prompted me to alert my three brothers, who lived several hours away. Recognizing the extent of her stroke, I knew Mama would no longer be able to live alone. Her cute two-bedroom cottage would not accommodate her need to use a wheelchair. I prayed my brothers would recognize and understand her needs.

After four weeks in the hospital, Mama, who was now seventy-five, agreed to move from the rehab unit of the hospital to the Inn at Southern Pines. I could now supervise her care. I promised myself that I would not break beneath the increasingly heavy load.

Exactly four months after Mama had her first stroke, I received another frightening phone call.

This time it was from Daddy. Because he never called me at work, I knew he was in trouble.

"Deb, I can't breathe. I need to see the doctor. Send Bo to help me... now!" Daddy knew my schedule was always too busy for my own good. Therefore, it was no surprise that he asked for Bo's help. Indeed, Bo had rescued him many times before.

With so much on our minds, it never once dawned on either of us to call an ambulance. While Bo was gone to rescue Daddy, I did finally pick up the phone and call his pulmonary specialist. Several years earlier, he had been diagnosed with emphysema after years of smoking cigarettes.

Daddy was admitted to the hospital with bronchial pneumonia, but even several rounds of potent intravenous antibiotics did not eradicate the problem. His doctor ordered an MRI and then a biopsy of the right lower lung. As a former oncology nurse, I wasn't surprised when the final report revealed a deadly diagnosis: small cell lung cancer—a fast-growing tumor that shows no pity.

After nearly three weeks in the hospital, Daddy moved to a nursing home, situated next door to the oncology center, while he received chemotherapy. After twelve treatments, the side effects had taken their toll. Daddy decided to stop the chemo and move to Southern Pines. I knew his stay would be a short one.

As I contemplated Daddy's move, a feeling of dread began to build in my stomach. Mama and Daddy had been divorced for twenty-six years and had never spoken to each other that entire time.

I recalled the unpleasant experience I endured during my college commencement exercise, just two months after their divorce. With Mama sitting on one side of the auditorium and Daddy on the other, I rushed to and fro trying to devote equal time to each of them. Now I could picture myself doing it again, all these years later, on the campus of Southern Pines.

With Mama now residing at the Inn, the only prudent decision was to settle Daddy in the Community at Southern Pines. For weeks, amid my stressful days, I shuffled back and forth between their rooms.

My new role as their caregiver naturally added to my already long list of duties, but another, even greater challenge demanded my attention. To finance their health care, I needed to sell their separate residences, their vehicles, and decide on the disposition of their personal belongings.

With a prospective buyer for Southern Pines demanding my attention, Mama receiving care in the Inn, and Daddy dying with lung cancer in the Community, I felt as if I were drowning by the weight of the additional responsibilities. Yet, I knew I had to keep going. If ever my parents needed me, it was now.

In the forty-two days Daddy lived at Southern Pines, he and I enjoyed many heart-to-heart talks, and during that time, he assured me he was ready to meet the Lord. He had accepted Christ while listening to a televangelist a year earlier. Daddy also shared his deepest struggle with me: a heavy codeine addiction that resulted from his never-ending back pain.

After multiple back operations that brought no relief, he turned to codeine. With Daddy in his final stage of cancer, I could only imagine the massive doses of morphine it would take to numb the excruciating pain.

He and I also discussed the magnitude of the project I

had undertaken as well as the scope of my responsibilities. He repeatedly encouraged me not to overwork—a character trait he recognized in himself.

"Life is short, Deb. You need to take time for yourself and your family," he reminded me daily. "You have an awesome responsibility here. I've seen it for myself. You never sit down. That worries me. I believe you're a workaholic!"

Two weeks later, after pulling another all-nighter, I strode the long hallway that led to Daddy's studio apartment. As I grappled with an envelope I'd received minutes before via overnight delivery, I could see a smile creeping up the corners of his mouth, dimples showing in his cheeks. The long-awaited news had finally arrived—a "Letter of Intent to Purchase." I'm not sure who was more relieved, he or I.

"I'm so glad you finally made the decision. You'll never regret it. Take some time off after the sale, just you and Bo. If you decide later you want to go back to work, then find a part-time job. But let this business go. Now!"

Exactly one month later, on a chilly fall Saturday afternoon in early October, Daddy died, but only after reminding me just a few hours before "to take care of Mama." I was honored to give the eulogy at his funeral. I faithfully shared memories and Daddy's words of wisdom with family and friends. Even today, his wise counsel remains ever so close to my heart.

Although the months of caring for Mama and Daddy were tough, the year was a memorable one for me. An amazing thing happened two days before Daddy's death, when Mama asked if she could visit him. I pushed her wheelchair to his apartment.

In spite of his sedated state, he opened his eyes and asked me, "Deb, who is that woman in my bedroom?"

With my voice cracking, I softly answered, "Daddy, it's Mama. Is that okay?"

"Yeah, yeah, yeah," he answered softly.

The tone of his voice assured me everything was well. For the very first time since their divorce, with Daddy lying on his death bed, my parents finally made amends—at Southern Pines.

Following this emotional encounter, I made my way to Wade Chapel and quietly slipped into a pew: the one named in my family's honor. There I immediately felt a sacred sense of quietude. As tears filled my eyes, I whispered a prayer thanking God for reminding me that He was there all the time, even during the most overwhelming and wearisome experience of my life.

Mama graciously agreed to attend Daddy's funeral. She sat in the reserved section with our family, and as his former wife of twenty-six years, allowed her name to be listed in the obituary notice in the local newspaper.

As the sale of Southern Pines drew nigh, an incident occurred involving my mother and another resident.

A male resident suffering from early Alzheimer Disease took a liking to my mom. Mr. Joe knew Mama was the 'mother of the boss'. He was adamant she was going to speak to him every single day. Being the strong-willed person Mama was, she was equally determined no one, not even Mr. Joe, was going to make her do something she didn't want to do. Though the staff and I tried hard to explain to Mama the importance of a simple hello, she refused to have any communication with the older fellow. Mr. Joe's demeanor continued to aggravate Mama to no end.

My mom had become quite independent following her divorce from my dad over twenty-five years earlier. She was a lady with her own agenda. And that is precisely what caused me concern. In addition to the residual effects from the stroke, I knew Mama's potential. When duty called, she could stand tall with the best of them.

Then it happened: One sunny Tuesday morning Mr. Joe passed Mama in the hallway. Instead of his usual hello, he approached in a straightforward way. "Why don't you speak to me?" he asked. With a few colorful words, Mama told him a thing or two. Before the staff could halt the discussion which quickly went south, Mr. Joe raised his walking cane and gently rested it in the center of Mama's chest. That was just enough to push Mama over the edge. A tug-of-war ensued. Mama took hold of Mr. Joe's cane. As he held on tightly to his cane, she let go of her end. Mr. Joe landed on the floor. Right there in the middle of the hallway. An ambulance was summoned. Mr. Joe's family was notified. The diagnosis was confirmed: Fractured left hip. Sadly, that injury led to complications that took Mr. Joe's life.

Southern Pines' policy was very clear: Residents who are involved in an altercation resulting in injury to another resident will be relocated from the facility as soon as possible. No questions asked! Though it was my mom involved, I knew my policies *had* to stand.

I immediately notified my brothers. They understood the seriousness of the matter. For the first time in my twenty something years of long-term care experience, I faced an 'inside' business dilemma that would affect my entire family.

So many thoughts crossed my mind: How do I explain the incident to the family of Mr. Joe? After all, his sweet daughter was Kyle's music teacher several years ago. How do I explain to the prospective buyers? There could be legal ramifications. I could see mounting paperwork staring me in the face. How will I tell my mother she has to leave her home *now*? Where will I place her?

The truth of the matter was, Mama either liked a person or she didn't. Not surprisingly, since her divorce, most of her hostility was directed toward males and that included residents. Who was to say she won't feel the same way about another resident in another facility?

This incident seemed far bigger than my weary body could handle. As I lay my head on my pillow that night and reflected on the events of that horrible day, my tears were lost in my prayer. Only God could give me the clear direction I so desperately needed.

The many friends Mama had made at Southern Pines begged me to reconsider my decision to relocate her. They became angry at me. They had no clue that I was obligated to follow my own policies. I had no choice.

Three days later Mama went to live in a beautiful, locally owned assisted living residence in a neighboring town, thirty minutes away. Bo and I ended up traveling one hour to and fro every other evening to visit Mama. That was in addition to my already packed schedule.

Before the owners of the new retirement home would accept Mama, I was required to sign a binding document. Following my explanation of the recent episode at Southern Pines, they were clear in their response: "You may be called to move your mother without the usual thirty-day notice if she shows any signs of aggressiveness." I fully understood their rationale. I had those same policies in place at Southern Pines. Besides, I had a clear understanding of the business side of owning and operating an assisted living facility and now I had a close-up, front row view of the personal side of caregiving!

The owners of the new facility didn't trust my motive for relocation of my mother. They only knew I owned a very successful facility fifteen miles away - maybe I was there to scope out the competition. I became aware that I couldn't relocate Mama to this, or any other nearby facility, without revealing the pending sale of Southern Pines. *How would I ever explain to the families of prospective residents? What would people think? Lord, I desperately need Your guidance.*

Each time Bo and I visited Mama at the new facility, she would cry. When we took her out for dinner, she couldn't enjoy it. Instead she cried. Though she quickly made friends at the new facility and was loved by everyone, she simply wasn't happy living outside of Thomasville. I felt sandwiched between a rock and a hard place. Each time we drove off leaving her behind at the beautiful assisted living facility, I felt a fresh stab in the center of my heart. *What should I do? What direction should I take? What options do I really have?*

Although I knew in my heart I was making the right decision, both for Mama and for the business, it didn't make the days any less traumatic. Those last five months, awaiting the sale of Southern Pines and tending to my mother's care from such a distance seemed like forty forevers.

To this day, I well remember the demands that went

along with being a responsible business owner. I vividly recall the heartfelt decisions that went along with serving as primary caretaker for my mother, while running my own assisted living residence. It was this difficult business decision that almost cost me my sanity and so affected the lady so near and dear to my heart: My mother; my very best friend!

Six months after building Southern Pines, I had been determined to move across the street to the Puzzle Lake Subdivision, a location that, at first, proved beneficial. In time, it became a liability.

Nearly ten years later, a resident's family member (Bill, an ER doctor, and his wife, Carol) expressed interest in purchasing our Puzzle Lake residence. They both had an idea that the sale of Southern Pines would prompt us to consider relocating. Besides, most of our friends thought we would likely wind up in the Smoky Mountains of North Carolina at Bantam Bend. With Mama's condition, we realized that the move to North Carolina wasn't about to happen.

Bo recognized that the decision to sell Southern Pines was firm in my mind. But he also understood that the decision to sell our personal residence was not a settled issue for me. The mere mention of leaving the home we had completely gutted two years earlier and had rebuilt to our specifications was agonizing for me.

"I love our home, Bo. Especially our beautiful custom knotty pine kitchen cabinets with the rooster cutouts," I reminded him as my tone escalated. "And what about the walk-in closets I designed for each of us and my custom dressing table?"

"I'm sure we can find another house you'll love just as much."

"No, Bo. You don't understand. I don't *want* another house. Just because the business is sold doesn't mean we *have* to leave our home. I'm not going anywhere!"

Bo said no more. He was concerned that another major decision at this point would push me over the edge. His physical and emotional support had been my lifeline, keeping me afloat during what had become the longest year of my life.

Because Carol's mother had recently moved from a Victorian cottage to a garden apartment due to declining health, Carol relished the thought of living in close proximity to Southern Pines. For that reason, she never let go of the idea that she and Bill truly wanted to buy our house. The minute Bo and I agreed for them to just "look" at our home, Carol fell in love with it! Each time she came back for a re-look, I felt my heart race as I wrestled with the thought of giving up another prized possession—my home—that had so much of "me" built in it. Ultimately, we did sell our home to Bill and Carol. We closed on the property exactly two weeks after the closing of Southern Pines.

During the previous three years, Bo and I had strayed from faithful church attendance. I simply did not have the energy to get up, get dressed, and go to church after working incessantly the other six days of the week. Instead of attending church, we watched televised messages by Dr. Ronnie Floyd and Dr. Charles Stanley as well as making time for on-line devotions. The numerous programs held at Southern Pines also helped meet our spiritual needs.

Several months before the closing on the sale of

Southern Pines, the buyers and I discussed an appropriate time to alert the residents of the impending sale. To that end, one month before the tentative closing date, I scheduled an important family council meeting.

I dreaded the event, as I knew it would be emotionally wrenching to say farewell to those I loved so much. In fact, I seriously wondered if I had enough reserve energy to deliver my talk.

Once I shared the news with the group, I felt a huge sense of relief until the tentative closing date passed with no papers signed. After two months passed, I experienced serious concerns. Daily I faced residents and staff asking the same question: "Is the sale really going to happen?" My anxiety level reached an all-time high!

I finally presented a pleasant ultimatum: "My partners and I will extend the contract fifteen days. After that, the sale is off." Those words forced the buyers to finish the legal work or walk away.

Five days before the deadline, I received official notice from my attorneys and from the buyers: The changeover would take place at *twelve midnight, June* 14, 2005.

---

"If anyone does not provide for his relatives, and especially for his immediate family, he has denied the faith and is worse than an unbeliever."

*1 Timothy 5:8*

# Chapter 27
## Early Retirement

"It's only when we truly know and understand that we have a limited time on earth—and that we have no way of knowing when our time is up—that we will begin to live each day to the fullest, as if it was the only one we had."
*Elizabeth Kubler-Ross*

Just as I begged to know the appropriate time to sell Southern Pines, I longed to *know* what my future would hold. *How will I stop work so abruptly? What will I do with my free time? Am I really ready for the title of retiree?* Like many business owners, my work was my identity. I was never asked who I was, but rather, what I did.

The morning after the sale, Bo and I awakened before the alarm clock. We had a lot of loose ends to tie up, so we set out early.

As a general rule, we personally delivered the quarterly publication of *Mainstreet Messenger* around town. Today we proudly delivered the final issue—a special edition recapping our ten years in business. As always, the office staff happily placed a stack in their waiting area. For me, it was one final chance to personally say thanks to those who had supported my endeavor. This time it turned out to be an all-day venture, but it was worth it because it brought closure.

Two days after the closing, Bo and I attended my retirement party held in Mainstreet Plaza Restaurant. As hard as it was, the words of Ecclesiastes 3 were the final words I shared in my last talk.

"There is a time for everything and a season for every activity under heaven, a time to be born and a time to die." My comments continued: "There is a time to buy and a time to sell, a time to hold on and a time to let go."

Before a large and enthusiastic crowd, I was recognized for my contributions to Southern Pines. I proudly uncovered a gorgeous, heavy bronze commemorative plaque, twelve inches by eighteen inches, that would later be placed in one of the courtyards at Southern Pines.

Inscribed were the words:

*This garden is in honor of Debbie Griffiths, R.N.C*
*Founder of Southern Pines Retirement Community*
*By providing the Thomasville community*
*with such a lovely choice for*
*"Retirement Living at Its Finest," she has*
*generously shared and inspired*
*countless residents, family members, and*
*friends with her philosophy*
*"Don't Regret Growing Old—It's a*
*Privilege Denied to Many."*

As I started to leave, I collected two spiral books laying on a table in the mall. Inside of one were words written by residents. One spoke ever so deeply:

> *Wow, what a little lady! I know you can't buy enthusiasm, loyalty, or the devotion we have for you! You've earned our hearts, our minds, and our souls. I pray you'll enjoy traveling with Bo to many wonderful places the world has to offer.*

The other one contained thoughts from various staff members. Two in particular touched my heart:

> *I want to thank you very much for allowing me to work at Southern Pines and for teaching me so much over the years. I believe that you can do anything you put your mind to. And you also have me believing that of myself! It's been a great experience for me.*

> *I can say it's finally the end to a new beginning for you and your family. Thanks for building such a wonderful place for all of us to work. You have completed your dream. I'm going to miss you coming at night… with your nightgown on. But I hope… some nights you will come to visit. I will always look up to you. In the February 2004 Mainstreet Messenger, you wrote something that caught my eye: 'My challenge to each one is to find your own uniqueness and build upon it in some special way.' What I like most about you is that you gave it your all—your very best, and that's what I want to do also.*

In the coming weeks, I knew their words would be a comfort as I faced the sadness of saying good-bye.

Unfortunately, Mama wasn't able to attend my retirement party. She was hospitalized, facing the possibility of a below-the-knee amputation.

After a quick celebration dinner, Kyle headed back to college in Americus, while Bo and I hurriedly made our way to the hospital before visiting hours ended.

There sat Danny and Rehberg, along with our bike-riding buddies, Reverend Gary Holland and his wife, Susan. I could tell Gary was bursting with news. The minute we walked in, he took one look at Mama and said, "Miss Pauline, tell Bo and Debbie what just happened." Unsure of what he meant, I saw the same puzzled look on Bo's face that was on my own.

Mama tried desperately to gather her thoughts then erroneously said, "I joined the church." Realizing he needed to help her explain, Gary spoke up. "No, Miss Pauline, you didn't join the church, but you did something far more important. Debbie, your mother accepted the Lord just a few minutes ago." Mama nodded her head yes with tears misting her eyes.

Immediately my thoughts raced back to the many times I and others had prayed for her through the years. With a knot in my throat, all I could say was, "Praise the Lord!"

Just as we left the hospital room and made our way to the elevator, there stood my doctor friend, the one I had phoned ten years earlier. I was touched when he congratulated me on my early retirement. "I just want you to know how proud of you I am," he said. While I regretted that he never accepted my invitation to invest in or dine at Southern Pines, I was gratified to know he appreciated my contributions to our local medical community.

Following that quick conversation I couldn't wait to get home. I wanted to call my friend and coworker, Miss Vera, to tell her my good news: "The day of my retirement party is the day my Mama accepted Christ!"

The next morning I completed the last business details as I disbursed the final paychecks and bid each employee farewell with a warm embrace. That very same morning the incoming director informed me that the residents' petty cash would not be transferred to the new company. I spent the afternoon at home calculating the cumulative petty cash monies for the seventy residents. The following morning I deposited the full petty cash amount in the Southern Pines bank account. And within five days I had written a final letter to each of the seventy residents (or their responsible party) explaining why I was returning their petty cash. The letter was mailed along with a Southern Pines check for each individual's petty cash amount. Although a very time-consuming process, this experience proved beneficial. It was just one more opportunity to provide closure for me.

I arranged a meeting for Bo and I to meet with Phillip and Joel, financial gurus working in the investment department at our bank. We spent three hours together discussing our financial future. My uneasiness was real, and the younger advisors listened intently to my concerns. Though on the surface it may appear that I'm financially secure, I am plagued with 'Bag Lady Syndrome' – a phenomenon that affects many women. I grew up on the wrong side of the tracks, so I needed to be sure that what I had worked so hard to earn would not be placed in a highly volatile portfolio. Bo is eight years older than I, and statistics show I'll outlive him by seven years. I must plan for widowhood.

"Bo and Debbie: we've carefully considered your income requirements. We've honored your wishes by taking a conservative approach, covering your needs while allowing for principal growth. Because you two are frugal, I don't see a problem. After eight years of full retirement, we're projecting that Debbie will reenter the work force. Knowing her, she'll be ready."

For my partners, once the sale ended, they were finished. However, they were kind enough to reward me with a cash bonus they had agreed upon from their share of the sale proceeds.

For me, the next two years meant handling the closing duties: record-keeping responsibilities, tax filing, and insurance and labor reports. I willingly honored the two-year noncompetition clause requested by the new owners.

Now that the two years have passed, I can honestly say I never experienced seller's remorse, as many thought might happen. For me, even today, the best part is going to bed each night and waking up the next morning knowing my contributions have made a significant impact in my hometown community.

Southern Pines, now under the leadership of its new parents, completed its expansion of *Phase V*—The Villages at Southern Pines—twenty-five independent-living apartments and two additional Victorian cottages. It's no wonder my hometown continues to grow as a Mecca for retirees.

As I look back, I recall a quote from the October 1999

edition of the *Mainstreet Messenger*: "Whenever one takes steps to pursue a vision that God has ordained, resources from everywhere help accomplish that vision."

In retirement, I can see clearly the numerous individuals who helped me along my path. One particular individual, Don, my former boss from Mulberry Place, the one who delivered the yellow envelope, offered sound advice just four months before he succumbed to an early death. His words of wisdom were in regard to my early retirement: "Debbie, make sure you hire someone you can trust to help you and Bo plan financially for a lengthy retirement. After all, you are mighty young. And by all means, don't forget to use your talents somewhere." Fortunately, our paths did cross again.

Although Southern Pines isn't my business anymore, and I'm essentially retired, I find tremendous enjoyment from helping others realize their dreams: Pinecone Management Company allows me the chance to use my talents in a variety of ways.

Deep within my heart, I truly believe that I am where I am today because of Mickey. I successfully built a premier retirement community, and I realized my dream along with the rewards of early retirement. The experiences I faced during Mickey's life and after his death prepared me well for a purposeful journey.

---

"It's a very short trip. While alive, live."
*Malcolm Forbes*

# Chapter 28

## In God's Will at RoosterVille

"Teach me to do your will, for you are my God;
may your good Spirit lead me on level ground."
*Psalm 143:10*

When I found retirement, I found peace.

For the first time in my life, I was fed up trying to justify my overly busy lifestyle. It had literally consumed my life. It was now time for me to think about myself first…just once. I truly didn't realize how difficult that would be.

I'd halfway made up my mind. Maybe it was time to let go of our Puzzle Lake home. Nearly every evening after work, Bo and I rode the streets in our town looking for another house. Sometimes our friends, Gary and Susan, joined us. Not only did it take our minds off the longest year of waiting, but it was relaxing. We had considered relocating permanently to the mountains, but with Mama's fragile health, that simply wasn't an option.

What we really sought was a place of privacy. "If we can find a house with a long, paved driveway, set back from the road, then I think I could let go of Puzzle Lake," I told Bo. We came close with three different properties; however, each time the deal fell through. I told myself: *Maybe it wasn't meant for us to move after all.*

Then out of the blue, at 10:30 p.m. on a Friday night, Gary called. Surfing the Internet, he stumbled across a house and property that had just come on the market. I assured him we would pursue it the following day. "But if this one isn't right, then I'm not looking anymore," I told him. "I'm tired of making life-changing decisions!"

On Saturday, Bo and I rode our Gold Wing in a parade with other bikers. As soon as the parade ended, we went in search of the property, looking exactly where Gary had specified. We even asked a builder in the vicinity, but there was no "For Sale" sign visible anywhere. Thirty minutes later, we finally saw it. The driveway was hidden by the thick foliage. Bo drove down the asphalted lane. No one was home. We peeked in the window of the smaller house. "I could use the dining area as my study," I told Bo excitedly.

"I really love this, Deb. I could live here," he quickly agreed. "And it's enough acreage to keep me busy."

For the first time in our house-hunting days, we finally found a property that *really* thrilled us both. In fact, we were so excited that neither of us slept that night. The modest, down-to-earth brick house was exactly what we wanted. Not too big. Close to town. The small one-bedroom guesthouse and the Dutch barn were also part of the package. "The arrangement is perfect. When my brothers come to visit Mama at the nursing home, they can stay in the cottage," I told Bo.

Between the dark green wood fence aligning the front

property and all the foliage, the surroundings were indeed private. In our minds, Bo and I were already making plans to add a privacy gate—a single green gate to match the fence with two roosters welded right in the middle.

Not wanting anyone to know of our interest, Gary initially followed up with the real estate agent. The following morning we revealed to the agent that we were the interested party. We were heartsick when we learned that a contract was pending. However, the agent said she would have a final answer on the pending offer by four p.m. the next afternoon. We diligently prayed for an open door if this was God's will for us.

At 4:05 p.m. the following day, the agent called. The previous deal had fallen through. At this point, we learned the house was owned by an ER doctor and his wife. We were next in line. Meanwhile, a lady in a Mercedes, a potential buyer from out-of-state, sat patiently in the driveway waiting while we were inside taking a second gander. Bo couldn't wait to tell her the house was "under contract." That night as we crawled into bed, we couldn't help chuckling. God had done it again!

Exactly four weeks after the business sale, we moved to the new home we named RoosterVille. Using the identical paint colors in our Puzzle Lake residence, RoosterVille soon became beyond-my-dreams perfect. All of our former inside furnishings fit the new house to a T. I could even use my favorite window treatments.

The buyers of our Puzzle Lake residence also requested to purchase our four wrought iron barstools. We used those proceeds to buy new twin padded barstools and a jelly cabinet. Other than that, we literally didn't have to purchase another item to furnish RoosterVille.

*Since our very first home together, Bo and I have tastefully decorated using a country theme with roosters and chickens. Today a population sign with "1892" hangs directly underneath the RoosterVille sign at the gate entrance. Many of our friends joke with us about our "Rooster Museum."*

*The sign at the gate of our new home, RoosterVille*

As we left the attorney's office following the sale of our Puzzle Lake residence, my phone rang. A couple from Atlanta wanted to buy Bantam Bend! There was only one stipulation: They wanted to close on our log cabin in six weeks! Bo and I worked hard to make it happen, and the closing finally took place on our twenty-fifth wedding anniversary.

In two months, we had sold Southern Pines, our Puzzle Lake residence, and the cabin, and moved to RoosterVille. We brought our favorite belongings from Bantam Bend to furnish the guesthouse we named Bantam Inn. All the rest we left for the Habitat for Humanity resale store in North Carolina.

Things hadn't slowed down a bit. Bo and I decided it was God's way of allowing me to transition without an abrupt stop. Just as with most addictions, change doesn't happen overnight.

While I awaited the move to RoosterVille, I jotted down a list of my retirement goals: Each started with an S: Simple, Seek, and Share.

For me, *simplifying* my life meant having and wanting less. Not feeling unfulfilled or dissatisfied, but rather getting back to the basics—like still using my old 1986 Tandy computer to keep up with the family finances. With the sale of Bantam Bend, the goal of simplifying had begun.

Nearly three years had passed since Bo and I cooked meals at home. In earlier years, he had cooked the meat on the big green egg while I prepared the trimmings. I longed for those times again, days when I could quietly sit on the front porch or watch a movie together with Bo and Kyle. I'm slowly learning the simple ways of life again.

I knew RoosterVille was the ideal place to *seek* God's will. It took my past experiences to teach me. I promised those I love that I'd never let busyness rule my life again!

I knew I wanted to *share* the blessings, such as giving back to those who helped me get started thirty years ago. Bo and I annually fund the Debbie Griffiths Scholarship to help students pursue an education in gerontology or nursing. At this writing, four students have successfully completed their education.

Although I still find public speaking a challenge, I realize I need to share my story, not just for my own healing, but to inspire others to follow their dreams and to find purpose after loss.

I almost declined an invitation to be the keynote speaker at a recent college graduation. I almost refused to address the state GOAL finalists in Atlanta, even though, at the age of seventeen, I was the youngest GOAL award recipient in the history of Southwest Georgia Technical College. Not only that, but I was also reluctant to serve as guest speaker at the very first gerontology graduating class. I even almost declined the invitation to share my testimony at the ladies ministry.

Then I remembered my three retirement goals: *Simplify my life, seek God's will, and share the blessings!* I simply have to share my story. I gave the speeches. I wrote this book.

---

"One of the most tragic things I know about human
nature is that all of us tend to put off
living. We are all dreaming of some magical rose
garden over the horizon—instead of enjoying the
roses blooming outside our windows today."
*Dale Carnegie*

# Chapter 29
## Little Lady, BIG DREAM

"I will not die but live and will
proclaim what the Lord has done."
*Psalm 118:17*

Everyone has a story to tell. Going through papers one day, I found a ten-year-old letter stashed away after long ago corresponding with a professional editor. I always knew I'd write my story, I just didn't know when. Finally, retirement has allowed me my chance.

I coveted a quiet place—just for me—to read and study, a place I could think without interruption. A place I could safely store my favorite books, journals, papers, and scrapbooks.

I decided on a tree house. Not a typical one in tree limbs above the ground, but one nestled among the trees on the back property of RoosterVille, where I escaped to write this book. It looks a lot like an old one-room schoolhouse and is a gift to myself. The tree house is not only my haven for expression, but it's my place to be alone with God and with myself.

*My haven (tree house) where I wrote this book*

I've written professional newsletters. A two-paragraph story of my first experience as a nurse was published in *Nursing* 1979. My brief testimony is published in the June 1994 *Decision.* I wrote the senior ministry biographies while teaching Sunday school, and I also submitted an article in the 1990 summer issue of *Resource*, suggesting ideas for senior adult activities. After all that, the thought of writing my life story unnerved me. I wondered what memories might unfold.

Then I reflected for a moment on the words of Dyann, my faithful cook at Southern Pines: "Miss Debbie, you should write a book. Your story about the beginning of Southern Pines is so wonderful. You need to share it."

The first day I sat down to write, Sandra's words echoed in my mind: "There is always an underlying reason why people work endlessly." At that point, I had to find out why I'd been so compelled to work.

As soon as I began writing, my feelings began to pour out like a flood. In my subconscious were many painful memories, repressed for decades. Incredibly, the more I wrote, the more I understood myself.

The truth is, empty spaces always fill with something. In my case, passion for work filled that cold dark hole that had begun so long ago. That passion led to my purpose for living, and in fact, work became my protection. Work shielded me from the inner demons I didn't know existed. Early retirement forced me to deal with the baggage I had avoided all my life. In writing this book, I learned to face those hurts in a straightforward way while simultaneously changing my outlook on life.

Spirituality is one of the first things recovering people regain, Sandra told me. In the quietness of RoosterVille and in the solitude of my tree house, I let go of the adrenaline rush that had filled my hectic life. I let go of all that I had bottled up inside. I slowed down long enough to hear the birds sing and to enjoy the beauty of nature.

Then I discovered my new passion—writing. I reclaimed an intense emotional excitement as my enthusiasm for life returned. Once I started writing, I found it difficult to stop.

When I recognized the addiction once again rearing its ugly head, I paused to get back on track. Work addiction will always be an ongoing battle for me, but I gave up night shift work the day I sold my business.

A few months after we settled at RoosterVille, I was invited to attend a weekly ladies Bible study. I heard the same comments everywhere I went: "I can't believe you sold that beautiful retirement community. How could you?"

Last year I had difficulty answering that question

without feeling guilty. Today, without the least bit of self-reproach, I can honestly answer, "To find myself and to return to my family."

I am finally "awake" in my life. I know what's important. I now have more of myself to give to others. I have come to value my difficult life experiences, and in this journey called life, I am now able to move on to fulfill other dreams.

Life's chapters begin and end then begin again. As simple as it might sound, I found it healing to trade in my white Town and Country Chrysler van. It looked so much like the Southern Pines vans. Bo and I even made the decision to sell the royal blue Gold Wing trike. I found a new breakfast location as well. Just one more attempt to begin again.

Bo and I also joined the Trinity family, a new church fellowship where I rededicated my life to Christ. This smaller church allows us the opportunity to give more and to do more. Finally, I have rediscovered my identity and have given myself permission to begin a new chapter.

Each Monday morning during my quiet time, I make my weekly "do for others" list. It's my way of constantly reminding myself of the needs of others, whether it's mailing a simple card or making a much-needed phone call. I enjoy volunteering in whatever capacity I can be of service, particularly in my local church.

In light of my new personal revival, I now ask myself these six questions before I tackle any new challenge:

1. How will it impact my family, my schedule, and my sanity?
2. Does it fit this "season" of my life?
3. Is it consistent with my gifts?

4. Is it a godly pursuit or a self-centered one?
5. Do I want to do it to serve God or to impress other people?
6. If this is to become a *precious memory*, what do I need to contribute to make it so?

Though still a *little lady*, I am much stronger now. I have the gift of a new perspective; I know what to embrace and what to let go. Just as I gave to every resident who entered my doors a little booklet called *Living Long and Loving It,* I, too, am able to reap those same benefits. In addition, I'm finally able to cast a vote for myself—without having to work myself to death.

---

"Your vision will become clear only when
you can look into your own heart.
Who looks outside, dreams;
who looks inside, awakes."
*Carl Jung*

# Chapter 30

## Move, Move, Move

"One must never lose time in vainly regretting the past or in complaining against the changes which cause us discomfort; for change is the essence of life."
*Anatole France*

For more than twenty years, Bo and I spent every Independence Day grilling, serving, and entertaining our residents and their families at the retirement community. This Fourth of July was different. Because Southern Pines had recently changed ownership, this was an Independence Day that we could finally celebrate on our own.

After a quick stop at Dairy Queen for a vanilla cone, we moseyed down the road in Bo's white Ford pick-up. Parked in the Gateway Shopping Center lot, he and I sat quietly enjoying the magnificent display of fireworks sponsored by the local utilities department. We relished the solitude. There was no way of knowing what lay just around the corner.

Two weeks earlier, Bo and I had moved all of my personal belongings, including some cherished items given to us by the new owners of Southern Pines, to our home in Puzzle Lake. Just ten days later, Puzzle Lake was sold, and we moved to our new home at RoosterVille.

Because Mama's health had declined, she was now in desperate need of skilled nursing care. Our plan was to relocate her back to Thomasville. In her healthy days, when the topic of nursing homes was mentioned, Mama always said she wanted to live at Camellia Gardens Nursing Home. Knowing we had chosen this exact facility made the anticipation of her move less stressful for me.

Mama's doctors informed us she had less than six months to live. She faced a ton of medical problems. Since I expected her lifespan to be short, I chose a private room for Mama. I was content knowing her social security income, as well as the proceeds from the sale of her home, would easily finance a six month stay at the nursing home.

After the first month's statement, I realized I had either misunderstood the costs of services stated by the admissions coordinator, or I had been misinformed from the outset. I expected the difference in the private rate versus the semi-private rate to be a mere $300.00. When the statement arrived, I discovered the difference was *$600.00 more* per month! I was appalled, since that was more than Mama's social security income. I chose not to overreact. As long as Mama's money was available, I expected her to enjoy everything she deserved at this stage of her life: A private room, weekly hairdresser appointments, nice clothes, new shoes, and outside opportunities. Whatever she needed or wanted, my desire was to see that she got it.

Mama wasn't allowed personal furniture at the nursing home, so we had to find an alternate location for many of her belongings. Reluctantly, I ended up selling most of it, since none of the family members needed the items. The cash went to Mama's care.

Bo drove the truck to Thomasville and I drove my car filled with Mama's smaller, more fragile items. While driving east on Highway 84, I was reminded of the words I had prayed shortly before I retired: "Please allow my mother at least two more years of quality life." Since both of us had basically worked our whole adult life, especially those last few years at Southern Pines, I looked forward to the absence of a work schedule, and planned to take Mama on a vacation with me. Mama was already in her late seventies and not in good health; I realized a gift of two more years was highly unlikely. Nevertheless, whatever extra time God gave us would mean the world to me.

Fourteen months in a private room quickly drained Mama's bank account. I made the decision to relocate Mama to a semi-private room. It was a wise and frugal course of action...or so I thought!

Mama would be sharing a semi-private room with a sweet, kind lady; a former elementary teacher. Each time I visited Mama, I'd speak to Ms. Jones. The staff and I were convinced this was the perfect roommate for Mama.

At first Ms. Jones and Mama got along like two peas in a pod. Unfortunately, Mama was easily bothered by anyone who disrupted her Friday night television programs, especially championship wrestling. Ms. Jones was bossy, often talking to Mama as though she was a student.

Over time, Mama became antagonistic. On several occasions Mama made it clear: "If that woman doesn't shut up and stop treating me like I'm one of her young'uns, I'm going to shut her up!" I knew Mama was dead serious!

The nursing home policy regarding aggressive behavior was the same as my former policies, so I couldn't help but become alarmed. *If I don't get her out of here before something happens, I'll never be able to find a place that will help me take care of my mother.* I stressed.

Immediately, my mind reflected back on that horrible incident with Mr. Joe during my last days as owner of Southern Pines.

I learned from the social director there were no available semi-private rooms with a compatible roommate for Mama. My instinct told me I needed to make a move—quickly! I allowed my heart to dictate my actions.

After some minor rearranging in our guest cottage, the decision was made: Mama is coming to live at RoosterVille. She had always referred to our guest cottage as a "doll house" so she was thrilled beyond words when I shared the news with her.

"But how will you manage her, Deb?" Bo questioned. "I think Granny requires more care than you realize, but I'll support whatever decision you make."

"Oh no, Bo, I'm a nurse and I *can* take care of my mother. I'll give her some chores to do, like keeping the front porch swept off and folding clothes. She will be a tremendous help to me. Besides, Bo, every time I visit Mama, the situation with Ms. Jones leaves me with a feeling of dread building in my stomach."

No one, not even Mama's sister, Aunt Wilma, could talk me out of this decision. My brothers tried. My son tried. But I didn't listen. It was my duty. *Why couldn't the men in my life understand my decision?*

Bo knew that I wasn't physically or emotionally ready to provide full-time care for my mother—even with his devoted help and support. Southern Pines had been sold, but now I'd be delivering care on the grounds of RoosterVille. The whole idea petrified Bo. He knew I hadn't recovered from the past twenty-something years of daily caregiving.

Three weeks after Mama's arrival, I realized I had made a poor decision. Mama wasn't safe in the cottage alone. The first week she overran the toilet and flooded the bathroom. The following week she neglected to turn off the stove after boiling water for her coffee. Her tiny, frail hands didn't even have the strength to lock or unlock the outside doors.

"What should I do now?" I asked Bo. The nursing home had no available semi-private rooms. I couldn't rest. I worried. And Bo, in his sweet, caring, and loving way answered: "I don't know what to tell you, Deb. But I do know you *must* do something. I'm concerned about Granny as well as your well-being. Remember *your* motto: You can't help others if you don't help yourself first."

The next day I contacted my friend, Gail, the director of a local facility. With open arms she welcomed my mother. I not only moved Mama's belongings in, but also decorated her room with splendid holiday décor, Christmas tree and all! Was Mama satisfied?

"I want to go back to Camellia Gardens. I heard a resident passed away last night. Go check and see if I can get the room with Ms. Perry." Another move! I took down the tree and the decorations and moved the small items back to Camellia Gardens. This time I hired a mover to transport the furniture to storage. Neither Bo nor I had the energy to make the complete move on our own.

Little did I know the move back to the nursing home would be the best decision I'd ever make for Mama. Not only did she desire to spend her last days there, she literally flourished. She became 'Queen Bee'; she was loved by the residents, staff, and volunteers alike. Each night a group of ladies played cards, and Mama soon earned the title of Rummikube champion. For the first time since the initial stroke, my Mama was happy as a lark! And when she was happy, I was thrilled beyond words!

Ms. Perry ended up being the absolute perfect roommate for Mama. "I pray I won't outlive her," Mama told me time and time again. That's how much she loved her new friend. More heartwarming was the fact that Mama became something of a caregiver for Ms. Perry who was suffering from late stage of Alzheimer Dementia. Life for Ms. Perry meant holding onto her baby doll and occasionally voicing a sound. When Ms. Perry's baby would fall off the bed, Mama was there to pick her up. When Ms. Perry was sick, Mama was the first one to notify the nurses.

A few weeks after Mama returned to Camellia Gardens, she faced a rare cancer on her right eyelid. Three operations at a specialized hospital were necessary. She was concerned her facial features would be altered from the surgery, but handled it like a trooper.

Four years later Mama was confronted with a dozen or more major surgeries to remove blister-like sores that popped up over various parts of her body. Radiation treatments followed. It was this rare form of skin cancer,

Non-Hodgkins Lymphoma of the skin, that produced massive tumors which ended her life on 6.11.11.

Not only had Mama become a caregiver during her time with Ms. Perry, she also was like a second mom to her roommate's family, especially her two daughters. The day Mama passed away, Ms. Perry's family grieved almost as deeply as my family and I. While delivering the eulogy at the funeral, I could see the faces of the two daughters, tears streaming down their cheeks. We each were the recipient of an answer to prayer. Just as she prayed, Mama went to heaven a year ahead of Ms. Perry.

As with my Dad's funeral seven years earlier, I was honored to share words of wisdom with family and friends at Mama's funeral. I included a list of 'Things My Mom Taught Me': Never give up. Be content in whatever circumstances I face. Have fun and laugh at myself. Take *One Day at a Time* (Mama's favorite song, sung at her memorial service). The epitaph: 'One Of A Kind' along with 'Love, Laughter, Life' engraved on the slab covering her grave, described Mama's life to a T.

Looking back, I have no regrets regarding the promise I made to Daddy hours before his death. "Take good care of your Mama," he told me. Though I tried desperately to take care of her in the dollhouse, I simply couldn't. With all the medical conditions, including that horrible cancer that took her life, there is no way that I, a burned out long-term care nurse and business owner, could possibly have met all of her needs. But I have peace knowing I did my best.

Following Mama's death, I received a beautiful letter from her sister, my Aunt Wilma: "*Debbie, I truly want you to know you looked after your mom when you were here. You hired help when you were not here. You did a good daughter job. Your mom was always dressed well. If she needed shoes, you bought them for her. You both were very close to each other over the years. What a big God blessing. You should have no regrets. Without Bo you would not have been able to do so much for her."*

Though I asked specifically for two extra years of quality time with my Mama, I was given six years. Even today I'm still praising God for that *threefold* blessing!

---

"Delight yourself also in the Lord,
And He shall give you the desires of your heart."
*Psalm* 37:4

# Chapter 31
## Speechless

"Success is all about achievement of
goals even where obstacles exist!
It's how we meet those challenges that matters."
*Anonymous*

I'll never forget that rainy Thursday afternoon in early August 2007. I had recently finished the second year of paperwork that followed the sale of Southern Pines. Three weeks earlier, on July 19, *Little Lady, BIG DREAM* had been released at a beautiful afternoon reception held at Southwest Georgia Technical College, my alma mater. In less than a week, Bo and I would be celebrating our 27th wedding anniversary.

Sitting at my custom built heart pine desk in the comfort of my cozy tree house, I followed up on various emails I'd received for book orders, and answered questions from prospective readers. Hearing bits and pieces of a new author's interview on the Oprah show that emanated from the TV behind me, I began to reflect on my own recent activities. Having completed several radio, television and magazine interviews, I was glad things were finally starting to settle down.

Meanwhile Bo was piddling in his brown metal building, the one we refer to as his bear shop. His shop stood adjacent to my tree house and the entrances were only steps away from each other. Anytime I peered out my window, I could see him concentrating on the task at hand. Soon after he retired from the maintenance position at Southern Pines, Bo picked up the hobby of carving bears from tree logs using a chain saw. He went a step further and was now carving bears from tree stumps in the backyard at RoosterVille.

Suddenly the phone rang inside the tree house; a rarity, since calls generally came through my cell phone. A nice gentleman on the other end of the line identified himself. "This is Mac, I'm your DHL delivery driver; I'm at the front gate. I'm looking for a Debbie Griffiths. She has a package marked 'Extremely Urgent'." I immediately shared the gate code and instructed Mac to drive his big, yellow truck straight down the asphalted drive to the back of the property. "Look for the tree house and you'll find me."

"What could be in this package, especially one so urgent?" It had been more than two years since Southern Pines was taken over by its new owners. Though I had continued to received documentation from various sources, such as the Labor Department, insurance companies, and requests for employee recommendations, those letters had somewhat subsided.

Bo had joined me in the tree house by the time Mac arrived, and we chatted for a brief moment. "Moving on to the next stop," Mac shared. Bo, a twenty-five years UPS driver, related well.

I could hardly believe my eyes when I opened that thick envelope. In my hands I held a publishing contract for *Little Lady, BIG DREAM* from Tate Publishing Company, located in Mustang, Oklahoma! An accompanying letter informed me that only 4% of the manuscripts are chosen out of the tens of thousands received each year. Without one letter of rejection, *Little Lady, BIG DREAM* would soon become a national publication. I was speechless!

For the next few minutes, I sat quietly at my desk—consumed by the fact that my story would soon be available in more areas than I could even imagine. Though I couldn't fathom sharing my story with those outside of my hometown, I realized it was simply meant to be. *Maybe I was supposed to write my life story. Maybe LLBD will reach a lot of people.* Tears began to well in my eyes and I became beyond ecstatic!

Then it hit me. I must call Tim, my wonderful editor. Six weeks before the self-published release of *Little Lady, BIG DREAM*, I took Tim's advice and submitted my manuscript to a national publisher. Though initially reluctant, I finally decided to do it—just to get him off my case.

"Hello, this is Tim at Write Choice Services." Tim quickly suggested I slow my adrenaline-fueled speech down and lower my voice. He didn't seem the least bit surprised at the news. "I told you, Debbie. *Little Lady, BIG DREAM* is far more than a hometown story. It spoke to my heart and it'll encourage a lot of people who need it. I'm so glad you followed through on the submission of your manuscript."

According to the contract, Tate would provide a full marketing package which included bookmarks, business cards and posters, as well as create a new, more marketable book cover. An editor would be assigned to review my manuscript (again) and my story. I'd have the chance to add or make changes to the Tate published edition. There would also be an audio book. I couldn't believe what I was reading!

Enclosed in the packet was a personalized letter from the Director of Acquisitions: *"I was truly blessed by your book and haven't been able to put it down the last few days. I have not read a book that offers this kind of personal connection and relationship with the author in quite some time. As a reader, I get to know you page after page; I started to feel a very deep connection in your life. Readers will learn from your experiences and relate to what you have gone through in many ways. Your book was a joy to experience and we are honored to have you come our way. God certainly used an ordinary 'little lady' to do great things for Him."*

During the time I was writing *LLBD*, I made many new friends. Tim introduced me to Joe, a fellow author who also became part of the Tate family. Joe and I talked often, encouraging one another during the time we were writing our stories. In fact, we jointly made the decision: Let's fly to Mustang to read our *own* book for the Tate Out Loud project. Since Tate allowed eight hours of recording time, I knew I could read my story in that allotted span of time. I was also certain no one could read my story with the southern inflection that only I could provide.

During the editing process, I was thrilled to make another new friend: Kylie, my Tate editor, who on one occasion shared: *"I cannot tell you the emotions I had while reading your story. What an amazing life you have lived; a life that has brought much glory to God. Thank you for telling your story—all aspects of it—and from the bottom of my heart, I thank you for the love and compassion you have for the elderly."*

While I anxiously awaited my new book release from Tate, I received a phone call from the human resources director of a manufacturing plant located in a nearby town. Physicals and lab exams were recently completed by a medical firm for their 500 plus employees. A registered nurse was needed to counsel each employee. Duties would include checking the blood pressure of all those with hypertension, reviewing lab results, and teaching preventive maintenance in relation to the individual's health care results. I relished this opportunity: A two-week job, eight to ten hours daily. Soon I began my first consultant job since early retirement from Southern Pines.

Within days of beginning work, an aggravating hoarseness crept into my voice. I was certain it was the result of all day, nonstop talking. Returning home from work, I shared with Bo: "I almost couldn't do my job today. I haven't had laryngitis in such a long while. Oh well, I'll drink plenty of fluids tomorrow. Then it'll be the weekend and my voice can rest."

On Monday the same scenario resurfaced. "Does my voice sound different?" I questioned Bo. No soreness was present but thc hoarseness persisted. I knew something was very wrong.

Later in the week, I began to wonder if I'd be able to finish my job. Communication was becoming increasingly difficult. It hurt to converse. Without a voice, there was no way I could counsel employees or review their medical exams. If I could just finish my commitment, then I'd make an appointment with my doctor. I couldn't quit. That's not who I am.

Three weeks before the Tate release of *Little Lady, BIG DREAM* in August of 2008, the hoarseness reached an all-time high. My voice became a deep rasp. "I've always had a soft voice," I croaked to Bo. "It's time for the new book release and I can't even talk right; I sound like a man, Bo. Why is this happening to me?" Sadly, by the time the publisher was ready for the reading of *Little Lady, BIG DREAM* for the Tate Out Loud project, my voice was a mere whisper. The book reading, which resulted in 363 minutes of recorded voice, was virtually impossible for me. I was deeply disappointed. I cried.

My primary physician, who had tried several medications, suggested an Ear, Nose, and Throat referral. Lab work and other important tests were ordered to rule out autoimmune disorder. Ninety days later, and just two days before Thanksgiving, my doctor scheduled exploratory voice surgery. "All I can see with the laryngoscope are red lesions. It could be a vocal polyp, and I know I can fix that," he assured me. It all seemed so easy. I was up for the challenge. I was eager to get my voice back!

One week before the surgery, I was blessed to share my story with a group of caring and tolerant older adults from a local church. They understood my vocal difficulty. As I fulfilled my earlier commitment at their early November meeting, their patience and love was evident.

Following the removal of the polyp, I adhered to the regimen my doctor instructed: Absolutely no talking for two whole weeks. I counted the days until I could talk again!

The first day I was allowed to speak, I fulfilled yet another prior commitment: A book signing in Ellijay, Georgia. Later that evening I spoke at a Ladies' Christmas Dinner at a local church. Though my voice was weak, with the use of a microphone I could be clearly heard. For the first time in a very long time, I finally had my voice back and I was beside myself with joy!

One month later that stubborn hoarseness resurfaced. Vocal fatigue reared its ugly head all over again. Though I could start a sentence, I had difficulty completing it. Phone conversations were futile. My local doctor continued to order various tests, but he was unsuccessful at finding a proper diagnosis. With Bo's ongoing hearing issues and my voice loss, we became a frustrated twosome.

Shopping alone became a nightmare. Those who saw me in the stores and knew me from my working days thought I had become "stuck up." They had no idea I had lost my voice, and I had no voice to tell them! After another month of struggle, it became easier for me to just stay at home. Depression covered me like a dank, musty blanket.

After a year long struggle, my ENT referred me to a specialist at the Emory Voice Center in Atlanta. A second voice surgery was done in the summer of 2009. "Debbie, you had a rare and unusual polypoid laryngeal tumor on your left vocal cord known as a myxoma," the surgeon explained. "It was large, but thankfully, it was benign! A myxoma generally is found around the heart muscle or thigh. We've removed it, but it can come back. Don't hesitate to come see me for an evaluation anytime. Being a nurse, you know what to look for."

I still sometimes struggle with a raspy voice. Lengthy phone conversations are especially difficult. I was amazed when my doctor explained that most people use a different voice on the phone than in person.

My surgeon also informed me that vocal problems will likely be an ongoing issue. My first surgeon used a laser to perform the vocal surgery, leaving behind vocal burns and subsequently scars that can never be erased.

Bo and I had the pleasure of providing two small scholarships to the Emory Voice Center. It was our way of giving back, and showing our gratefulness to those who helped restore my voice and my life.

For the first time in my life I now understand that listening is a true art. Those quiet days allowed me the opportunity to search the Scriptures that focus on verses mentioning speech or voice. Proverbs 21:23 is now a favorite, and I cling to it: "Whoever guards his mouth and tongue keeps his soul from trouble". I value the simple wisdom that verse provides. I make every effort to choose my words carefully. And I have promised myself that I'd never again take physical health for granted, especially the ability to communicate.

Some time after the surgery and subsequent return of my voice, I had the opportunity to attend the Ladies' Christmas Party at the Blue Ridge church—the same annual event where I had spoken two years earlier. Sitting at a large round table with several other ladies, I overheard a conversation. A very nice lady shared. "I've never missed any of the Christmas parties held here at the church. My favorite program was the one where a *little lady* shared her story. She had owned a retirement home. Her story truly blessed my heart." Little did she know, that little lady with a BIG DREAM was sitting right beside her. Listening to her kind remarks, I found myself, in a good way, absolutely speechless!

---

"In the multitude of words, sin is not lacking,
but he who restrains his lips is wise."
*Proverbs 10:19*

# Chapter 32

## RoosterVille … Letting Go

"Change is often rejuvenating, invigorating, fun … and necessary."
*Lynn Povich*

Bo and I felt like we lived out in the country, though RoosterVille was just on the edge of town. With four acres surrounding us, there was always something to do; sometimes too much.

After living behind the gate at RoosterVille for nearly four years, Bo and I finally admitted to feelings of isolation and overwork. We longed for a change. Maintaining the primary residence, guest cottage, tree house, bear shop, red tool barn, front porch and a screened porch, as well as a huge deck and outdoor patio, in addition to the property, wasn't fun anymore. It was hard work, and Bo, now sixty-one years of age, was tired of the daily grind.

One evening while Bo was at the men's meeting at church, I sat on the back deck in my favorite wooden Adirondack chair, absorbing every single word contained in a book on work addiction. The more I read, the more

I could see myself. I learned alcoholic parents often produce workaholic children. Perfectionism and shyness are selfish traits often found in work addicts. Though I never once considered myself a selfish person, I began to recognize areas in my life that needed fixing. I immediately bowed my head, quietly asking God, first for forgiveness, then direction. Occasionally I still pull out that book. It reminds me, a known work addict, of my need for guidance. And that book leads me to the Book of books.

I remember an incident that is just as vivid today as it was on that fall day at RoosterVille. Walking from my tree house to the main residence, I stopped dead in my tracks in front of the cottage. I thought I heard a voice: "Get ready!" It wasn't audible, yet it was as clear as though someone had spoken directly to me. I responded out loud: "I'm trying to get ready." Exactly what I was getting ready for, I wasn't so sure. But I knew without a doubt that God was up to something. That very day I began the process of *rightsizing*: shedding material items we had accumulated in our twenty-eight years of marital bliss!

One bright, cheery morning in late April 2009, our realtor Carrie called. "Bo, I know RoosterVille is not on the market, but I'm convinced I have a buyer if you and Debbie will allow me to show your property."

The appointment for the prospective buyer to see the property was set for Saturday, five days away. Bo and I met the nice couple from Tennessee. Three days after their tour of RoosterVille, Carrie brought us an offer. The downside: Vacate by the end of the month!

More exciting news followed the *same* afternoon we received the offer on RoosterVille. Kyle landed a job with a large bank in Jacksonville, Florida, that would double his salary. It only made sense: When RoosterVille closes we will purchase Kyle's house! Of course, this new little house needed its own name. The offspring of RoosterVille was named 'The Chicken Coop'. Finally… a smaller primary residence, less upkeep, and an adorable log cabin. The whole idea felt lighter. Soon we realized though we had less, we really had so much more!

We loved our cabin in the Smokey Mountains but soon realized it could never be our full-time residence. We decided to sell it. Since we wanted to live *near* the mountains full-time, we considered our options. We immediately fell in love with a 55 and older active adult gated community: The Village at Deaton Creek located in northeast Georgia. In the spring of 2010 we purchased a home there.

A month later, an older couple signed a one year lease to rent Kyle's house, The Chicken Coop.

With the cabin on the market and The Chicken Coop leased, Bo and I were finally free to enjoy a busy lifestyle at Deaton Creek. We made new friends. Took square dance classes. Bo participated in the men's softball league. We visited in each other's homes. We went out to eat with friends. Life was good at Deaton Creek.

One Sunday we attended Blackshear Place Baptist Church. It took only one visit to convince us that's where God wanted us to serve Him.

The thirteen months we lived at Deaton Creek while attending Blackshear Place, brought tremendous spiritual growth to our lives. We also witnessed a remarkable numerical event at Blackshear Place. A third morning service, known as the 8:08 service was initiated. Bo and I attended the very first 8:08 service on our 30th wedding anniversary. That very day we joined Blackshear Place. The time was 8:08 and the date was 8.08.10—a historical moment we'd never forget!

Bo and I were able to sell the Smokey Mountain cabin only five months after listing it. We had already decided to donate the proceeds entirely to Blackshear Place to help build The Venue, a new youth center. We had not yet tithed following the sale of our business. We knew it was God's money, but we hadn't received clarity where He wanted us to give it. Since we loved our new church and could see the fruits of labor happening before our very eyes, we were certain this was *the storehouse* where we were to contribute. Believing strongly that the young people of today are tomorrow's church, we were thrilled to invest in this huge vision.

On the other hand, the adversary wasn't pleased. The realtor made a mistake with her percentage of profit, creating havoc afterwards. Later, we discovered a huge bank error. The audit department only deducted 10% of the total check amount from our account, rather than 100%. The remaining monies stayed in our account for nearly six weeks. Temptation reared its ugly head: "Bo and Debbie: just leave it alone, you guys gave the contribution, the church has the money and the bank will never find the error." But we resolved to correct the error, and it took grueling, daily visits to the bank to do so. It was clear: **Satan did not want The Venue student center to be built**. One year later, at the very first Venue service, 34 first-time salvation decisions were made, along with ten surrenders of those committed to full-time ministry!

Having a part in the 'Reaching Generation Now' project changed our life. We knew we could never outgive God!

Now that the cabin was sold, I continued with my rightsizing project—determined to shed more earthly valuables. Letting go of the cabin meant *less* to maintain, *more* to invest in what really matters!

It was only two months later that I received the first phone call from Mama's doctor, telling me the seriousness of her situation. Suddenly I felt an overpowering urgency to return home. My mother needed me. I wanted to be there. I made five trips home during the last month we lived in Deaton Creek. I wanted to move back home.

Leaving northeast Georgia was a very hard decision. Leaving Blackshear Place was an even harder decision. But the thought of not being present during my mom's last days was unbearable for me.

Our heavy heart was lightened by our Pastor's kind letter: *"Bo and Debbie, I have not been able to get your recent email about your move back to South Georgia off my mind. I am sad you are leaving. I am thankful for the brief time the Lord has allowed me to be your Pastor. I have also been praying for you in these future days of transition. May the Lord's favor continue to rest on your lives. You two will always be dear to my heart! I love you!"*

The cabin was gone, Deaton Creek was sold, and our renters back home decided not to sign another lease. Hooray, no longer a landlord! Six weeks later, we were back at The Chicken Coop. For the first time in a very long time, we were the proud owners of *one* property—the most liberating feeling in the world! I finally understood the meaning of that audible voice, "Get ready" way back when. Shedding a ton of stuff early on, helped immensely with all the moves. I was back home.

Just ten days after our move back, my mom died unexpectedly. That night, I answered the phone to hear a familiar voice. "Debbie, this is Jim, your Bible Fellowship teacher from Blackshear Place. Brother Dave and I are sorry we didn't make it in time for the visitation. May we visit with you in your home?" In an instant, that moment sparked a gentle reminder of the love and compassion Bo and I felt the minute we set foot in Blackshear Place a year earlier. The 600 mile round trip our Christian brothers made to support us in this time of loss confirmed the fact one more time: Blackshear Place was the church fellowship God intended for us.

Though the move to and from Northeast Georgia (all within a thirteen month period) was difficult, I wouldn't change the circumstances for anything. Spending Mama's last days with her meant the world to me. The final four days, even while she laid unresponsive at Camellia Gardens, provided personal satisfaction that only I, her one daughter, could know and experience. I'll always be grateful to her doctor for his wisdom: "Your mom has only a few days left to live, Debbie. She'll be listening for your voice, so stay close." And that I did.

---

'If you always give, you'll always have.'
*Chinese Proverb*

# Chapter 33

## The Lavender Book

"May the Lord bless you ... All the days of your life;
And may you live to see your children's children."
*Psalm* 128:5-6

Being back in South Georgia at The Coop presented new challenges. Many of the local residents thought we moved back to repurchase Southern Pines. Since the retirement community had been bought and sold numerous times, rumor had it: Bo and Debbie are back! In fact, The Coop was only meant to be a temporary home.

After a busy lifestyle at Deaton Creek, things at The Chicken Coop were quiet. Too quiet! When our friends were not working, they wanted to be at their own homes. They spent weekends catching up with household chores, just like we did when we were working. I soon discovered retiring at a young age brings its own issues. For the first time since my retirement, I had time on my hands.

Though Bo and I loved living near the mountains, we determined we would not relocate again without first selling The Chicken Coop—regardless of how long it might take.

Bo kindly planted two gorgeous topiary hibiscus—one red and one peach-colored—on either side of the front porch, in memory of Mama. They were sent for the funeral service by close friends. I began to realize life without Mama would never be the same. The emptiness in my heart would never go away. Each morning I opened the window blinds and stared at the lovely hibiscus. Sometimes I'd say: "Good morning, Lord; good morning, Mama."

We did a lot of extra cleaning in the yards, removing years of underbrush. We added a beautiful white vinyl fence near our neighbor's house. White pickets were added across the back of the carport to match the side fencing. We stayed busy while awaiting the birth of our first grandbaby– a girl—due in August.

*A kiss for BaBo and DebBo's special Valentine!*

Exactly two months after Mama's death, Baby Kelsey Elan Griffiths was born in Tifton, where her mommy, Stephanie, was employed as a registered nurse. I was overjoyed when Stephanie invited me, along with her mom and cousin, to witness the birth of our precious granddaughter. What a miracle to see a baby born, especially my own grandchild!

Bo and I were thrilled with our new roles: Babysitters! Keeping Kelsey and spending time with our sweet next-door neighbor, Brooke, who also had a baby girl (Edie, born just twenty-seven days ahead of Kelsey) became our lifeline. The four of us girls, along with Bo, spent hours together sitting on the porch at The Coop.

The first ten months we provided much of little Kelsey's daycare. The bonding that took place is among some of the best moments of our life. Now Bo and I know firsthand what we had always been told: "Grandchildren are the greatest gifts a child can give to their parent."

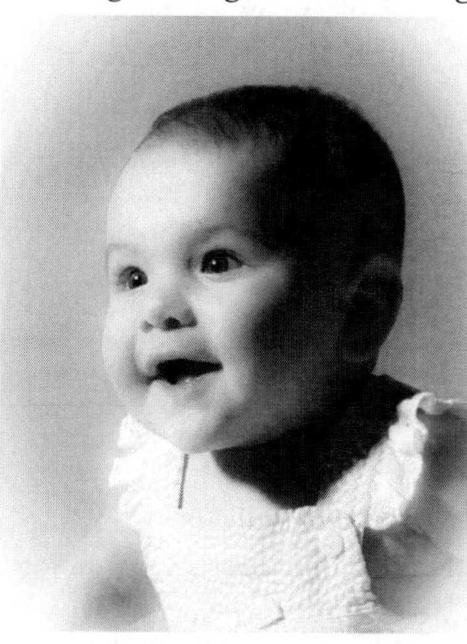

*Baby Kelsey: The Apple of our Eye*

The days we didn't keep Kelsey, we discussed our future plans including where we wanted to really retire. We decided the location of our *final* move: Either Jacksonville, where Kyle and his family would be living *or* return to Flowery Branch, where we were deeply connected. No doubt we would not remain in southwest Georgia. Living in or near a large city would give us plenty to do.

"Deb, I'm praying the Lord will just send the right people to buy the Coop," Bo proclaimed. "I just believe He will when He's ready for us to make a permanent move. It's an adorable little house, perfect for a retirement or newly married couple, and I think someone is just going to drive up and ask to buy it."

"Yeah, right!" We both giggled.

"How would anyone know we'd even consider selling, Bo? There's not even a sign in the yard!"

But soon after that front porch conversation, an amazing thing happened. Out of the blue, on a sunny Saturday, just before lunch, a young couple drove up in a silver sports utility. "Mr. Bo, I'm Kyle and my dad is Jeff. This is Stephanie, she's my bride-to-be. We heard you may be moving. Could we please look at your house? We've searched the area for months without success."

In the meantime, I'm in the background analyzing the situation: *Wow, another Kyle & Stephanie?! How bizarre is that? God, is that really You?*

I looked at Bo, totally speechless, my eyes as big as saucers. "Yeah," Bo sent a small grin my way, "Probably next spring we'll be moving to Jacksonville or to the mountains. But you two can take a peek now if you like." I stood behind Bo, nodding my head yes....and remembering his prayer!!!!

"Mr. Bo, we're getting married in 6 weeks. We hope to have a home by then." My jaw dropped!

The minute the couple walked inside they fell in love with our little Coop. "Just seeing those beautiful green kitchen cabinets confirms it. This is the perfect house for us. We want it!"

Six weeks later, Kyle and Stephanie White owned the Chicken Coop. We had no idea where we were going to live. Fortunately, the precious couple allowed us to stay in their home four weeks after the closing, at no charge. In return, we surprised them with a beautiful black wooden entertainment center.

Decision-making time! After talking with our Kyle and Stephanie, we learned they may not remain Florida residents. Bo and I realized we needed direction. *We can't keep moving to accommodate the needs of our family. I wish I had learned that a long time ago. On the other hand, we can't just leave baby Kelsey! But we'll have Face Time several nights each week along with regular monthly visits to Jacksonville... It'll be okay!*

We took our scheduled family vacation the following week. Coming back through northeast Georgia, we spent four days with an agent searching for the right home in the right location. The landmark: Blackshear Place. We wanted to be near the church and close to the area where our friends were. Deaton Creek was out. The truth is, living there for thirteen months felt like being at Southern Pines. I was simply not ready for this style of living—no time soon!

We had fallen in love earlier with the homes in Reunion Country Club—just two miles from Deaton Creek. One reservation: Only two and three-story houses were available. Rightsizing was still fresh on my mind. We were pleased when the realtor informed us a new, smaller model home was available at Reunion. "The Forsyth model may well provide the perfect layout for you two," she said. "It's 1800 square feet with a master on the main. The upstairs is 1050 square feet, space for the kids when they come to visit." We decided it was all part of the plan. We took it.

*Our newest ride, the Can Am*

We also purchased a brand new three-wheeled motorcycle—a white Can Am. Touring the mountain roads with our church biker group, 'His Thunder Riders' adds to the fun of retirement.

Not long after we settled from the move, Bo and I drove to the Lifeway Bookstore across from the Mall of Georgia—one of our favorite spots to hang out. I quietly browsed the aisles while listening to the sound of lovely music from the overheard speakers. Turning the corner, I caught a glimpse of a gorgeous lavender book. I wanted to hold it in my hand. It was absolutely beautiful!

As I drew closer, I admired the unique leather cover. The bottom half was smooth to touch. I envisioned my new title: 'Gran Deb' engraved right smack dab in the middle. I ran my hand across the upper portion of the cover, feeling the embossed flowers, designed like lily petals. An ivory stripe divided the two sections. Then I spied the words that melted my heart: 'The Grandmother's Bible.' Ahhhh! I must show it to Bo. *I'm taking it home with me!*

When I opened the lavender Bible, I was more convinced. On the left inside cover was a plastic pouch—the perfect location for a picture of my little Kelsey. I made my purchase, excited to get home and review the detailed interior.

I was thrilled when I discovered just what my new Bible included: 365 devotions, one for each day of the year, to help nurture my Christian walk. Presentation pages to record events about Kelsey. Perspectives related to grandparenting. Stories to share with Kelsey. Life lessons and talking points. A prayer at the end of each devotion. My new Bible would be teaching me ways to continue to be a positive influence on my first grandchild.

During a weeklong visit to our house, Kelsey decided to give 'GranBo and GranDeb' new names: DebBo and BaBo! Easier for an eighteen-month-old to say! It's okay that my lavender Bible has GranDeb stamped on it—just one more story I'll have to share with her one day.

Though not yet two years old, she's plenty smart and no stranger to new places. After two visits to Blackshear Place with DebBo and BaBo, she traipsed the long hallway through the double glass doors to her Bible Fellowship class like a big girl. I want Kelsey to remember me like the Apostle Paul remembered his protégé, Timothy's grandmother, Lois: "I have been reminded of your sincere faith." (II Timothy 1:5a)

I have so much work to do to continue to prepare for

my role as grandmother. I can hardly wait to share the life lessons and talking points with Kelsey. I'm praying for her now and I know my lavender Book will prepare me well.

---

"His children will be mighty in the land;
the generation of the upright will be blessed."
*Psalm* 112:2

# Chapter 34

## Legacy Of Faith

Vision is not enough; it must be combined with venture.
It is not enough to start up the step;
we must step up the stairs!
*Anonymous*

Becoming a DebBo changed my life! During the first ten months of Kelsey's life, BaBo (Bo) and I had the privilege of keeping her in our home for up to fifty hours a week while her parents worked. While this angelic newborn slept, I worked to complete an enormous project.

For years I enjoyed creating memory books—the old-fashioned way. Cutting and pasting with colored, lead-free construction paper, I haunted Hobby Lobby and Michael's to find just the right stickers and decor. Any significant life event warranted a photo book to tell the story. The palest ink is better than the best memory.

I remembered the moving guys commenting on the heaviness of certain massive boxes. I never wanted to risk moving or damaging those bulky, oversized scrapbooks ever again, and became determined to find an alternate method to keep my memories close by.

*Baby Kelsey's first Easter - 2012*

Creating little Kelsey's "baby book" gave me the idea. Eight months later, thirty-five albums were rightsized/ converted to twenty-eight beautiful hard-back, storybook photo albums. Disassembling the old scrapbooks and scanning photos was a labor of love; I was determined to provide a "living legacy" for my Kelsey.

With one album devoted to each of my parents, Kelsey will *know* her paternal great grandparents. Five albums capture her daddy's life, from his birth to her birth. Several travel books reveal places she's been, as well as sights her parents and grandparents have seen. The story books of her DebBo and BaBo reveal the importance of hard work and sacrifice. The albums reflect a journey of faith. Kelsey will know where she came from. In each of her own photo books, she can read a letter written especially to her from DebBo. At this time, the library of albums is neatly displayed in a bookcase in our family room.

BaBo and I are setting up a Biblical audio library for Kelsey. A scripture, Amos 8:11, reminds us: "Behold the days are coming, says the Lord God, that I will send a famine on the land; not a famine of bread, nor a thirst for water. But of hearing the words of the Lord." If truth is someday taken from the doors of the church, perhaps she can listen to the Bible in her home.

And there's the lavender *'Grandmother's Bible'*—a tangible legacy. Hopefully, the handwritten notes inside will represent a progression of my faith, my desire to study God's word, and will be a positive influence in Kelsey's life.

You hold in your hands another part of my legacy—my spiritual memoir and life story, filled with amazing illustrations of God's hand at work. It's a story of faith, obedience, guidance, intention, perseverance, forgiveness, compassion, healing, and ultimately, fruition and success—in the midst of what appeared to be impossibility. *Little Lady, BIG DREAM* is a true legacy of faith for my family and a message of hope for my readers.

And finally... Will there be *Little Lady, BIG DREAM*, the movie? Yes, God willing! And this is how it all began ...

Along with two friends, I attended a preview screening of an upcoming movie.

While waiting for the movie to begin, I recalled a time, four years earlier, when I was contacted by a film guy about bringing *Little Lady, BIG DREAM* to the screen. I loved the idea, but I was deeply involved in the care of my mother. So it was an impossible task, an unlikely dream! I never gave it another thought.

At the end of the screening, introductions were made; accolades given. The usual applause. Then the film's screenwriter/director, Michael McClendon was introduced. While he stood, the audience raved, but I sat very still in my theater seat. I couldn't believe what I just heard. I didn't voice a word. *Is this a message for me?*

Since my fiance, Michael McLendon (Mickey) died nearly 40 years earlier, I'd never one time met or heard of anyone with the same name.

A month later I mustered the courage to email Michael McClendon, just to see if he'd take time to read *LLBD. Maybe he won't be interested.* I told myself. The truth is, I was eager to drop the whole idea.

In prior weeks, at least six new readers mentioned *LLBD* becoming a movie. Strange, since so much time had lapsed since its first release in 2007. Each time a *new* reader finished reading, I heard the same comments: "There's a message of hope. It needs to be shared on the screen!" *No way, I'm retired! I really wish people would leave me alone, including the screenwriter, the new Michael McClendon, who was now sending me positive feedback. Does he really believe LLBD needs to be shown on the screen? Is he for real?* Yet many signs pointed out the direction. Out of the blue, Michael commented to me, "Before I write, I always pray that God will establish my thoughts ----- Proverbs 16:3". No way! That IS the scripture I have written in every book I ever signed—except his! I had neglected to sign his book! He couldn't have known that. He couldn't have… *Lord, is this a sign from you?*

For some reason, I couldn't seem to drop this idea, though I kept telling myself that I wanted to. This began to seem familiar, and then it struck me: This is exactly how I felt about Southern Pines—should I build it or just stay comfortably where I was?

More pieces began to fall into place. I found that

Michael, the screenwriter/director, was born the same year as my Michael and they were both nicknamed Mickey. And they both have a brother named David. And Michael (screenwriter) had been deluged with script offers since the completion of his latest film, but *mine* was the story that interested him.

*Is this all just coincidence? I don't believe in coincidences… but I DO believe in signs. Spiritual warfare hammered in!*

Moving on to this project didn't feel comfortable; the movie business was completely alien to me. But God often shines His light mostly warmly on His children when they are *out* of their comfort zone. I prayed diligently, seeking guidance and direction.

Finally, the day before meeting with Michael, I sat listening to Pastor Jeff. His sermon concerned what people *do* and what they *neglect* to do. This felt familiar, like hearing Dr. Ronnie Floyd on TV while contemplating the start of my own business. Pastor Jeff's words echoed through the auditorium and into my heart: "Why are you just sitting here? Take a risk!"

I have the passion to share and I know real passion is the Holy Spirit.

Four months following the movie night with the girls, *Little Lady, BIG DREAM* is being transitioned into a major motion picture. I am in a strange and new land and my veins are pulsing with excitement. God's will is the desire of my heart. We shall proceed and see what happens.

Little did I know the urgency I felt to create the beautiful photo albums would also serve as a valuable tool in transitioning of *LLBD* to film. Michael uses my albums as inspiration. *A picture is worth a thousand words.*

Coincidentally (?) during the time of transitioning the book into a movie, Tate Publishing sent a letter asking if I was interested in having a second, expanded edition of *Little Lady, BIG DREAM.* All of these things just seemed to fall into place at the right time, but then, God's timing is perfect!

Maybe it was all in the plan from the very beginning. I lost my voice when *LLBD* was first released, but God had plans for a bigger voice to reach a bigger audience. I serve a very BIG God and *Little Lady, BIG DREAM*, the movie, will live on forever with a message of hope and a legacy of faith.

As I look back, I'm reminded of the ways I've been privileged to serve. Even today, the best part is going to bed each night and waking up the next morning knowing my contributions have made a significant impact in the lives of others. **That's a true legacy of faith!**

---

"You are never too old to set another
goal or to dream a new dream."
*C.S. Lewis*

# Epilogue

## My Version of Psalm 30

### Praise for Deliverance

I will praise you, O Lord, for you allowed me the reward of
early retirement and did not let my career get the best of me.
O Lord my God, I prayed to you for direction and you guided me.
O Lord, you brought me new owners from north Georgia;
you freed me from working twenty-four hours, seven days per week.
Sing to my Lord, as everyday I reflect;
I praise His holy name.
For my career lasts only a while, but His blessings last a lifetime;
burnout may remain for a time,
but God's strength comes in the morning.

When I felt overwhelmed, I said, "I will never be forgotten."
O Lord, when You molded me, You made my faith stand firm;
but when You shed a frown, I was saddened.
To You, O, Lord, I begged for a replacement;
"What gain is there in my business if I go down with poor health?
Will the success praise You? Will it proclaim Your faithfulness?
Hear, O Lord, and be compassionate to me;
O Lord, be my helper."
You turned my hard work into leisure time;
You removed my "on-call" status and clothed me with delight,
that my heart may share with others and not be afraid.
O Lord my God, I will express gratitude forever.
Amen.

# Afterword

When complimented by someone who insisted he was an extraordinary person, Theodore Roosevelt said, "No, I'm not an extraordinary person, only an ordinary man extraordinarily motivated."

God always uses ordinary folks to do incredible and wonderful things! To God, it's not about ability, but availability.

Debbie Griffiths is certainly one of those God has motivated in a most remarkable and extraordinary way—and because of her, He has changed many lives!

Garland Basford,
Minister
Thomasville Church of Christ

# Work Addiction Self-Test

To find out if you are a workaholic, rate yourself on each of the statements below, using the rating scales. Put the number that best describes your work habits in the blank beside each statement. After you have responded to all twenty-five statements, add up the numbers in the blanks for your total score. The highest score is 100; the lowest possible is 25. The higher your score, the more likely you are to be a workaholic. The lower your score, the less likely you are to be a workaholic.

Rate each statement according to the following scale:

1: never true
2: rarely true
3: sometimes true
4: always true

___4___ I prefer to do most things myself rather than ask for help.

___3___ I get impatient when I have to wait for someone else or when something takes too long.

___4___ I seem to be in a hurry and racing against the clock.

___4___ I get irritated when I am interrupted while I am in the middle of something.

___3___ I stay busy and keep many irons in the fire.

___3___ I find myself doing two or three things at one time, such as eating lunch and writing a memo while talking on the phone.

___2___ I over commit myself by biting off more than I can chew.

___4___ I feel guilty when I'm not working on something.

___4___ It's important that I see the concrete results of what I do.

___3___ I am more interested in the final result of my work than in the process.

___3___ Things just never seem to move fast enough or get done fast enough for me.

37

2 I lose my temper when things don't go my way or work out to suit me.

1 I ask the same question over again, without realizing it after I've already been given the answer once.

3 I spend a lot of time mentally planning and thinking about future events while tuning out the here and now.

3 I find myself continuing to work after my coworkers have called it quits.

2 I get angry when people don't meet my standards of perfection.

3 I get upset when I am in situations where I cannot be in control.

3 I tend to put myself under pressure from self-imposed deadlines when I work.

4 It is hard for me to relax when I'm not working.

4 I spend more time working than socializing with friends, or on hobbies or leisure activities.

2 I dive into projects to get a head start before all the phases have been finalized.

27

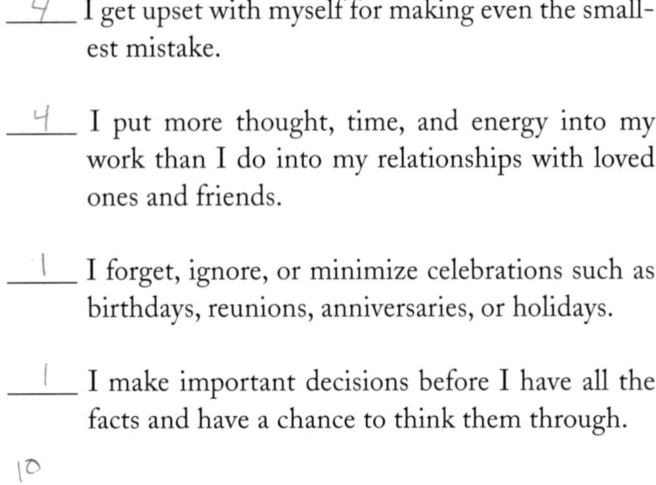

_____ I get upset with myself for making even the smallest mistake.

_____ I put more thought, time, and energy into my work than I do into my relationships with loved ones and friends.

_____ I forget, ignore, or minimize celebrations such as birthdays, reunions, anniversaries, or holidays.

_____ I make important decisions before I have all the facts and have a chance to think them through.

**SCORING:**

For clinical use, scores on the WART are divided into three ranges:

Those scoring in the upper third (67–100) are considered highly workaholic; if you scored in this range, it could mean that you are on your way to burnout. New research suggests that family members may be experiencing emotional repercussions as well.

Those scoring in the middle range (57–66) are considered mildly workaholic; if you are scored in this range, there is hope. With acceptance and modifications, you and your loved ones can prevent negative lasting effects.

Those scoring in the lowest range (25–56) are considered not workaholic; if you scored in this range, you probably are an efficient worker instead of a workaholic. You need not worry that your work style will affect yourself or others.

## PORTRAIT OF THE PHYSICAL AND BEHAVIORAL SIGNS OF WORK ADDICTION

| *PHYSICAL SIGNS* | *BEHAVIORAL SIGNS* |
|---|---|
| Headaches | Temper outbursts |
| Fatigue | Restlessness |
| Allergies | Insomnia |
| Indigestion | Difficulty relaxing |
| Stomach aches | Hyperactivity |
| Ulcers | Irritability and impatience |
| Chest pain | Forgetfulness |
| Shortness of breath | Difficulty concentrating |
| Nervous tics | Boredom |
| Dizziness | Mood swings |

Taken from: *Chained to the Desk–A Guidebook for Workaholics, Their Partners and Children and the Clinicians Who Treat Them;* Bryan E. Robinson, Ph. D. Copyright 1998.

---

"The work will wait while you show
the child the rainbow
but the rainbow won't wait while you do the work."
*Author Unknown*

---

"You can always find reasons to work.
There will always be one more thing to do.
But when people don't take time out,
they stop being productive.
They stop being happy, and that affects the
morale of everyone around them."
*Carisa Bianchi*

---

"The harder you work, the harder it is to surrender."
*Vince Lombardi*